# Ogham and the Wood Wide Web

## Using the Power of Trees for Divination and Magic

SANDIE COOMBS, DIANE MAXEY
AND WENDY TREVENNOR

GREEN MAGIC

Green Magic
53 Brooks Road
Street
Somerset
BA16 0PP
England


www.greenmagicpublishing.com


Designed and typeset by Carrigboy, Wells, UK
www.carrigboy.co.uk




ISBN 9781838418557




GREEN MAGIC

This book is lovingly dedicated to the beings
without which it could not have been written,
or any other book for that matter:
the TREES.

## ACKNOWLEDGEMENTS

The authors would like to thank
Mara Freeman for her kind permission to reproduce
her poem *A Druid Blessing for the Trees*.

Also Karen Thomas, who so diligently proofread
our work.

# Contents

# A DRUID BLESSING FOR THE TREES

A ninefold blessing of the sacred grove
Now be upon all forests of earth:
For willow of the streams,
Hazel of the rocks,
Alder of the marshes,
Birch of the waterfalls,
Ash of the shade,
Yew of resilience,
Elm of the brae,
Oak of the Sun,
And all trees that grow and live and breathe
On hill and brake and glen:

No axe, no saw, no fire shall harm you,
No mind of ownership shall seize you,
No hand of greed or profit claim you.
But grace of the stepping deer among you,
Strength of the rooting boar beneath you,
Power of the gliding hawk above you.

Deep peace of the running stream through your roots,
Deep peace of the flowing air in your boughs,
Deep peace of the shining stars on your leaves,

That the harp of the woods be heard once more
Throughout the green and living earth.

**Mara Freeman**
Reproduced by kind permission of the author:
https://www.chalicecentre.net/

Then, dearest Maiden, move along these shades
In gentleness of heart; with gentle hand
Touch—for there is a spirit in the woods.

*Nutting* **by William Wordsworth**

# How to use this Book

The subject of trees and their use in magic and divination is explored as thoroughly as we were able in the earlier chapters of this book. Finally, we come to the large section on the Ogham themselves, which covers facts on the trees – the mysteries associated with each one and the meaning and use of the Ogham for each tree.

You may wish to skip to the end and read that section first, but we recommend you take the time to absorb the information given in the earlier chapters afterwards, if you do not read them first.

# Introduction

The other day I went for a walk in some magical woods with two witches. One had recently been quite unwell and had been in hospital; as we entered the wood she took off like a rocket, all traces of weakness gone, and quite outpaced us younger ones.

Woods have this ability to rejuvenate and heal, to smooth away stress and anxiety, even to alleviate grief and anger. It is easy to see this at first as just the cool of the wood, which envelopes you as you enter, shutting out the heat of the Sun and insulating you from outside sounds. But as you linger under the trees, a dreamlike quality develops and you find your mind drifting in ways associated with the practice of meditation; the brainwave patterns change and the rhythms of your body seem to slow and strengthen. The magic of woods is there for all to experience.

Sadly, humans have abused and exploited trees, as they abuse and exploit all living things with which they come into contact, including their own kind. There are estimated to be just over three trillion trees on the Earth, which works out at 422 trees to every human being, a comforting figure were it not that we are only too aware of the way in which trees are disappearing. Horrific facts are thrown at us every day in the media: country-sized forest acres vanishing every day under bulldozers and power-saws to make way for crops or livestock grazing to feed the ever-increasing world population … or to satisfy its drug addictions. Now, with the planet and our lives on it critically endangered, we are beginning, a little belatedly, to realise the importance of these amazing and beautiful beings and the fact that they could save us if we let them.

Our ancient ancestors tended to have more respect for trees and for the plant kingdom generally; trees of one kind or another have been sacred to many cultures and in one instance have inspired a very special magical alphabet and divinatory system: Ogham. This beautiful and mysterious writing system is very much a part of the world of the Celts. Its association with the God Ogma points to its importance to the Celtic priesthood (known as the Druids) and their nature wisdom – their ancient and magical relationship with trees and with sacred groves which in its turn is very much still part of the British psyche and still as relevant today to those on a spiritual or magical path.

We three, all witches and one also a Druidess, have long felt close to nature and green things: it is part of the neopagan tradition, and now we have been inspired to put our heads together over the Celts' sacred Tree Alphabet. Come with us for a walk in the woods, explore the primeval forests of the mind, meet the beautiful and magical trees of the world and find out how they might communicate their wisdom to us.

*Wendy Trevennor*

# 1

# Ogham, the Tree Letters of the Celts

The Celts as a race have never been inclined to lie down under invasion and conquest by anyone, including the Roman Empire; from the real-life Boudicca to the comic book character Asterix, they have famously fought back with every weapon at their disposal. One theory for the creation of the Ogham alphabet is that it was developed deliberately as a private code that the Romans could not read. If this was true, it must have been effective; it embodies a completely different concept for lettering from the Latin letters we still use in the West, which were written one at a time, left to right, across a wax tablet or papyrus scroll in exactly the same way we write them today. Whilst modern handwriting may be stylistically joined up, printed letters are separate. Ogham works differently.

Ogham looks very alien and challenging to modern eyes because it was designed to be written along edges, around the corners of vertical stone pillars, wooden marker posts and doorways or, if on a flat medium, upwards along previously installed straight lines which rise as high as the medium permits before a fresh line is started to the right, again from the base of the medium. These continuous vertical lines, termed *ridges*, are then used for the placing of the letters, which are created by attaching between one and five horizontal strokes, either at 90 degrees either side of the base line, or at 90 degrees or sloping at the diagonal, right through it. The Ogham vowels also have a smaller form, little bullet-shapes, instead of full strokes. When inscribed on stones and posts, the actual corner of the stone forms the base line (the ridge) and the strokes of the letters are positioned on this, and thus often lie across two faces of the stone. No punctuation is used or any symbol to mark the divisions between words. It is hardly surprising that of the 400 or so surviving examples throughout the British Isles, there are a handful that have so far defied translation. Like Norse runes, the letters are composed of straight lines to make them easier to carve into stone or wood.

The letters, also called *fews*, are read from the bottom upwards – like climbing a tree – and the base of this line forms an inverted V-shaped "stand" which does look a little like the base of a tree where it widens out at ground level. The script would run from left to right, starting from the base of the leftmost ridge. Another V, an inverted one this time, is often added at the top end of the ridge to mark the end of the script. Later, when paper manuscripts were common, Ogham was occasionally adapted to horizontal lines to fit in with English or Latin inscriptions, so that a string would lie with its right side down and thus still be read from left to right. It is sometimes seen as margin notes made by a reader, for it is particularly suited for vertical jottings along the

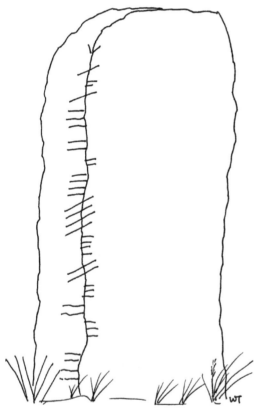

*Line drawing illustrating the use of Ogham around a stone's corner.*

edge of a page. Needless to say, Ogham has now made it into the twenty-first century and is available as a Unicode extension! As an example:

⟩‖••••‖／••‖‖‖Ⅲ••••‖‖⟨ = good morning!

Obviously, on a computer it can only be typed horizontally. See this Wikipedia page for details on how to use this Unicode extension: https://en.wikipedia.org/wiki/Ogham_(Unicode_block)

Originally there were 20 Ogham, consonants and vowels, divided between four *aicmes*, or families. The letter P is missing, for this was not a sound used in "Q-Celtic", or Goidelic – the strain of Celtic ethnicity that migrated from Europe into Britain and moved north or west to become the Scottish, Manx and Irish Celtic peoples (the Brythonic peoples who became the Bretons, Welsh and Cornish are called P-Celts, as they did use the letter P, but did not have Q in their language). Likewise, there is no Y or J. Yet the alphabet includes not only Q, which was used in the Gaelic languages, but the odd *few* (letter) Ngetal, which does not occur as a single letter-sound in English, but represents the sound NY or NG. Later, a fifth aicme of five more *fews* was added to represent diphthongs and other sounds.

What was Ogham used for? Most writing systems, from ancient Egyptian hieroglyphs and Sumerian cuneiform to Norse runes, were used by ordinary people (where there was a reasonable level of literacy) as well as rulers, administrators and priests. Examples can often be found of them being used for everyday jottings, messages, lists, inventories, love-letters and memoranda, as well as public announcements. However, Ogham does not appear to have been used in this way. The examples surviving to us are almost all of personal names (including a

*Sandie standing by the Ogham stone in St Martin's churchyard, Lewannick, near Launceston, Cornwall. The stone, now so weathered it is almost impossible to see the inscription, is believed to be a grave marker.*

person's status within his family and his tribe) and were used as boundary markers or grave markers. Quite a few of these inscriptions include reference to the individual's relationship to sacred trees, including phrases such as "born of hazel" or "son of rowan." The language used on the inscriptions is mostly primitive Irish, though a few examples of Pictish do occur, and it seems to be the very first writing system developed in the British Isles.

The identity of Ogham's Irish inventor or inventors is lost in the mists of time, for this writing system may be as old as two and a half millennia, although the earliest actual examples we have date from the fourth century CE. There are four current theories about its origins. The most popular states that it was designed in Ireland, to be indecipherable to the Romans (although no attempt to invade Ireland was made until 81CE, the Irish Celts must have been aware of the conquest of England). Most of the surviving Ogham inscriptions are found in Ireland, specifically in Munster, though they do occur across the northern and western regions of the British Isles. The early Christians are credited in another theory, which states that scholars wanted a unique alphabet that was custom-made for dealing with the Irish language. A third theory claims that Ogham comes from West Wales, where it was created as a way of reconciling the Latin writing with the Celtic language – the second largest number of examples is found in Wales. The final theory is that it was invented in Cisalpine Gaul, where it was used mainly in hand signals – the original four groups of five letters were presumably represented by the fingers and the separate joints thereof in some agreed way – and later came to be used in writing. As hand signals it could have been used as a secret language between Celtic peoples, one which invaders would be unable to understand, or perhaps even to recognise as a language. However, although putative systems exist for its use in this way, there is no archaeological evidence for this fourth theory.

There is also evidence in the *Book of Ballymote* of related systems of Ogham divination based on other signs in nature, including conogham: "dog-ogham"; dathogham: "colour-ogham"; boogham: "cattle-ogham"; enogham: "bird-ogham"; and several more. Exactly how these worked is not clear, but the idea calls to mind the traditional oracles in cultures such as ancient Rome, where the movements of birds and the intestines of slaughtered animals were inspected and read as signs.

Celtic legend credits the Irish and Scottish warrior God, Ogma, whose name seems to mean "cut" or "cutter", with the

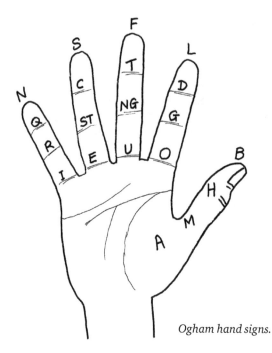

*Ogham hand signs.*

development of the letters. The term "Ogham" (which therefore possibly means something cut or incised) refers to the individual letters; the alphabet is more correctly known as Beith-Luis-Fearn, or Beith-Luis-Nion, the names of three of the letters, or the Beith-Luis-nin: Beith-Luis-letters (there is more than one way of ordering the letters, but we have gone with the most usual one, in which Fearn is the third letter). Ogma, termed "Sunface", was the son of the Dagda, chief of the Gods, and a member of the Celtic supernatural tribe Tuatha De Danaan. In classical terms, he relates better to Mercury/Hermes/Thoth than to the war Gods; his epithet *Grianainech* referring possibly to the light of his intelligence and the inspiration he bestowed on mankind. However, there is no tale to explain his creation or the reason for it, such as the Norse legend of Odin's discovery of the runes or Thoth's creation of the ancient Egyptian hieroglyphs.

The Celtic preoccupation with inspiration and especially poetry would have rendered Ogma a very important deity:

remember that in Ireland the most puissant chieftain would tiptoe carefully around any poet, lest he displease him, for the poet might then make use of his gift to blast him with a mocking or abusive ballad, or *aer*, which would not only destroy his credibility but would even be seen as capable of harming him through the magic of words, as an enchantment.

We have the *I, Claudius* author Robert Graves to thank for setting Ogham firmly on the table in the twentieth century for all to see, study and use after centuries of neglect and obscurity, and it has become an important tool and resource for neopagans, especially those drawn to Celtic spirituality. His 1948 book, *The White Goddess*, picked up concepts from the earlier twelve-volume study of comparative religion and myth, *The Golden Bough* by Sir J G Frazer, and ran with them. It has become a standard textbook and inspiration for pagans, and his theory of once universal Goddess worship having been displaced by Christianity – to the general disadvantage and woe of mankind – strikes a loud chord with modern pagans. The book contains an enormous amount of information about spirituality, poetry and legends from the Mediterranean to Western Europe and also explores Ogham, a system whose nature affiliations also strongly attract pagans. However, as he later admitted, Graves got carried away and invented for the system attributes it had never possessed, including the notorious "Tree Calendar". It is in the nature of scholars to speculate; Graves was no exception, and some of his ideas have been discredited. Sandie, a Druidess, says she had never read *The White Goddess* because of the many discrepancies within its contents. "Many Druids have read it," she explained, "some love it but are aware of the inaccuracies. I was never called by my inner self to reading it."

Whether the now traditional association of the Ogham with trees came later or was a part of the original concept is a subject for scholarly argument, with a modern theory stating that the tree associations were added later and that only eight of the

Ogham have tree names. However, the tree tradition dates back to the *Auraicept na n-Éces*, a textbook of Ogham from at least the seventh century CE, though scholars claim it was added to and tweaked up until the twelfth century.

We say to this: go with what you feel, belief is all. After all, if everyone were forced to scrap beliefs based on whether they were old enough and sufficiently original, Christianity would have lost a great many of its concepts, including the Assumption of the Virgin Mary, the divine nature and celibate status of Christ … and Christmas! All traditions start somewhere and most of them develop and change with the times and with the discoveries made by scholars and practitioners. The fact remains that even the Ogham which do not have clear tree names are smeared with moss and wound around with roots and twigs in a very deliberate and meaningful way.

The very language used of the Ogham is based on wood and trees: the individual letters are called *fid*, which means "tree", and collectively *feda*, which means "trees" or "wood". The Ogham and their parts are spoken of in tree terms, with each of the small lines that make up each letter and fork from the central line being called flesc, or "twig". This seems appropriate when you recall that the central line was originally written vertically, like a tree trunk, and the small sideways strokes of the letters sit on it like the branches of a tree.

Like the Norse runes, the Ogham had a system designed to help practitioners learn and remember them and their meanings. Where the Norse runes had the three Rune Poems, each version with a verse for each stave; the Ogham are set out in three ancient *Briartharogams,* word-lists, which are reproduced at the end of this book. These lists contain many kennings, little puns to add meaning, which often confuse rather than enlighten!

A further problem is that, while trees or shrubs have been assigned to the Ogham, in many cases these are quite unsuitable or unlikely – what, for example, is the vine doing in an Irish alphabet? It is not native to Ireland and clearly does not belong among oak, hazel, elder, birch and willow. How does the reed fit in with these woody trees? Or the ivy?

We have decided to hedge our bets, if you will excuse the arboreal pun, and both go with tradition and suggest innovations.

Ogham is of interest to students across the world, and why should those in other nations have to struggle with the difficulty of working with trees they have never seen or have the slightest connection with? Ogham inscriptions have been found across the world, including on ancient stones in the Americas and Canada, leading to the conclusion that Celtic traders and settlers made Ogham an international tool for their trade and for the spread of their religious beliefs and rituals, and of course British trees were not always represented in these climes.

Whilst British trees have been and always will be at the heart of Ogham, we feel all trees that live on Earth have their own magic and should be included in this work. Many of our trees are "foreigners", imported for parks and gardens and now naturalised, familiar and well-loved – what English village is without its horse chestnut, for example? How many London streets benefit from the imported London plane tree or the pollution-immune ginkgo? How many suburbs are without at least one Chilean monkey puzzle? So instead of staying self-isolating in the UK, our adventure will take in the beautiful trees of the world and their meaning to the ancient cultures to which they are native.

All trees are magical, all are potential saviours of mankind, bringing us shade, timber, fruit, seeds, clothing, medicine and, above all, oxygen. Let us celebrate them through this ancient divinatory and magical system which seems to have been designed to honour them.

# 2

# The Mystery of Trees

Of all life forms on the Earth, trees are some of the most revered and sacred in all cultures. All religions have a relationship with them, from the sacred acacia tree under which the Gods planned and created the world in Ancient Egypt, to the infamous Tree of Knowledge of Good and Evil in the Garden of Eden in Christian belief, and ultimately Christ's cross itself, which is often described as a "tree". The Egyptians also saw the sycamore or sycamore fig (Ficus sycomorus) as deeply sacred and even embodying the Goddesses Isis, Hathor and Nut, who are sometimes depicted in the form of this tree but sporting a human breast and suckling the Pharaoh with their divine milk. The Egyptians expected to see many of these trees, which bear succulent fruits in large quantities, when they entered paradise. The Druids planted groves of trees, which served as temples, and revered the oak, not exclusively, but above all other trees. The Norsemen saw the cosmos as a giant ash tree, with all the nine worlds, of men, of Gods, of giants and other supernatural creatures, suspended in its immense branches. A similar tree called Asvattha held up the cosmos in early Indian belief. The Buddha achieved enlightenment sitting under a bodhi tree (the sacred bodhi, peepal tree or Bo fig, Ficus religiosa), which has ever since been sacred to Buddhists in all countries, and also to Hindus and Jains. The Hebrew Qabalah is seen as a tree, with the ten Sephiroth hanging like fruit in its branches. In the Holy Roman Empire, the shade of a revered linden tree was used in place of a building to hold courts and assemblies.

Trees are deeply embedded in our subconscious, and not always in a very positive way: we tend to regard large conglomerations of them with basic fear and distrust, as is shown by the very commonest setting for traditional fairytale stories going back many centuries, such as Hansel and Gretel, Little Red Riding Hood and Sleeping Beauty. This primaeval forest grows in the deepest recesses of our minds and houses primitive fears.

In literature too trees have made their mark, from the two trees of Valinor in Tolkien's *Lord of the Rings* trilogy (and not forgetting the noble Ents, his tree-shepherd beings!) and the god trees or *weirwoods* in George RR Martin's *A Song of Ice and Fire* series, to much loved children's books like Enid Blyton's *The Faraway Tree* and the "whomping willow" in JK Rowling's *Harry Potter* books. The whomping willow appears in several of the movies as well, and other films have "starred" trees such as the designer-created Tree of the Dead in *Sleepy Hollow* (1999) and the terrifying animated tree-being in *A Monster Calls* (2016). Shakespeare, a country boy originally, loved them and used them in several of his plays, despite the difficulty of creating woodland on the stage at the Globe! They have inspired music, song and poetry, featured in the work of artists from Palaeolithic cave painters to Tracey Emin and prompted at least two art forms devoted exclusively to living trees: topiary and Japanese bonsai.

Christians (and many non-Christians too) have a real or artificial tree in the house over Christmas (a custom appropriated from earlier pagan culture) decorated with glittery baubles and sweet things. Boughs and twigs of holly and other evergreens are also brought inside to decorate the home, a custom that is so ingrained that it is almost impossible to see a holly leaf without thinking of Christmas. The old Norse custom of the Yule log continues, though today it is more likely to be made of chocolate.

Modern pagans often continue the ancient practice of hanging offerings on the branches of special or sacred trees, perhaps to ask favours of the tree, such as healing for a sick friend. Trees growing over or near holy wells will often be seen decorated with *clooties* (strips of cloth), crystals and even jewellery, though modern pagans generally ensure that any fabric used for this purpose is biodegradable.

Folk magic practice in many cultures has included petitioning trees for healing, or attaching small tokens, including facsimiles of injured limbs or sick babies, to its branches, passing a sick person through large holes in the trunk, and even injuring the tree itself so that, as it healed, the patient would also recover. Sometimes the illness was seen as being transferred to the tree, through the attaching of hair, clothing or other tokens.

While the trees thus honoured are generally seen as devoid of consciousness, they are usually seen as the homes of deities or spirits who would be offended and seek vengeance if the tree is injured. Classical mythology is full of dryads and hamadryades, as well as assorted nymphs and young men who have been turned into trees and shrubs for their own protection or for punishment. This type of belief has survived for many years and when Herne's oak, said to be the home of this mysterious spirit (now associated with the Horned God in modern paganism), blew down in 1863, Queen Victoria quickly ordered another one to be planted on the same spot in Windsor Great Park.

As well as life and health, the tree can also be associated with death in some cultures, as for example the traditional British churchyard yew and the historical Native American practice of sky burial – hoisting bodies, with or without coffins, into the tops of trees to decay. This was done for a variety of reasons, including avoiding the possibility of the disinterment of the body by animals, or because graves could not be dug because of snow and ice in winter. While many cultures across the world and throughout time have used timber for coffins, the Norsemen also used wood for their burials, building elaborate funeral ships in which their more influential dead were either buried or set adrift on the nearest body of water with their ship in flames. In the UK the practice of green or woodland burial has become more and more popular, especially with pagans: the deceased person is interred in a patch of land, often in a wicker coffin or other coffin designed to speed the process of decomposition, and a tree is planted on the grave. In Japan there exists the notorious "suicide forest" *Aokigahara,* said to be haunted, which is not surprising. This large area of conifers and broadleaf trees, including oaks, holly, birch and sycamore species, seems to draw in depressed and lonely people, who have committed suicide there by the hundreds over the years – although it could also be claimed that the influence of the trees is welcoming and soothing to deeply depressed, suicidal people in their last hours. Gibbets and gallows are often described as "trees" in historical fiction and accounts of executions.

As consciousness is the magic of humans and higher animals, so photosynthesis is a significant part of the magic of trees (but not the only part: see further down this chapter!). While all green plants produce oxygen through photosynthesis, trees outperform all other green things, due to their sheer size: a mature tree can have a quarter of a million leaves on it: that's enough to cover a football pitch if you laid them all out in a single layer. And of course, photosynthesis implies carbon capture, healing for our emissions-poisoned world, as the trees store this chemical away for centuries in the form of timber. For every six molecules of water they take in, trees take six molecules of carbon dioxide (the most prevalent and deadly of the greenhouse gases) and produce a molecule of glucose for their own sustenance, using no other resource than the light of the Sun. With this, and with other nutrients absorbed from the soil, these amazing beings grow from a tiny seed to a massive organism that can, in the case of the real giants – the sequoias, redwoods and *Eucalyptus regnans* (the swamp or stringy gum of Australia) – approach 350ft in height and have a basal trunk circumference of 100ft.

Their sheer size is impressive, but not the only reason trees have been universally used as landmarks. Because they can be relied on to be still in the same place after centuries (as long as humans do not cut them down), trees are the very best of signposts, easily visible and recognisable from some distance off and helpful even to those who cannot read. People in Cornwall value a beech hanger on elevated ground beside the A30 which has been celebrated in paintings and photography. Cookworthy Knapp is better known to most Cornwall residents as "the homecoming trees," as the copse suddenly appears in the landscape just before travellers heading west cross the border into the Duchy.

Trees easily outlive all humans, and even all other organisms on the Earth. A Great Basin bristlecone pine (*Pinus longaeva*) called the Methusaleh Tree in the Inyo National Forest, California, is known from timber sampling to be 4,853 years old (in 2022). Its location is kept secret for its own safety – an even older tree called Prometheus nearby was tragically felled in 1964 and was found to be at that time over 4,844 years old – that takes you back in human terms to an era before Stonehenge or the Great Pyramids of Giza in Egypt were built. A now deceased researcher in the area claimed to have found a living bristlecone that was well over 5,000 years old in 2009, but this is unverified. In the United States the giant sequoia, *Sequoiadendron giganteum*, is known to achieve great ages, and several specimens have been recorded at over 3,000 years old.

The Fortingall Yew in Perthshire is popularly supposed to be the oldest tree in the UK; its age estimated at between two and three thousand years, but there are other strong contenders for this title. The 60ft-circumference yew in St Cynog's churchyard, Defynnog, Wales – where there is a fine example of Ogham carvings on a stone in the church porch – may be even older: recent DNA analysis suggests it is more than 5,000 years old. The Crowhurst Yew in Surrey, which sports a wooden door into its hollow base, is said to be 4,000 years old. A yew tree at the National Trust property of Ankerwycke in Surrey, is known to be at least 1,400 years old, and believed to be as old as 2,500. At Marton in Cheshire a huge sessile oak is thought to be 1,200 years old. An old English saying states that mighty oak trees take "500 years to come, 500 years to stay and 500 years to go," giving them a total life-expectancy of a millennium and a half. To a tree, human beings might seem like flies; our lifetimes passing in the blink of an eye compared to the longevity of the tree, which has seen governments rise and fall, buildings go up and fall again, many generations of people live and die.

The importance of trees to the human race and to life on Earth generally can hardly be overstated. A human being can live for weeks without food, for days without water, but only for minutes without air. Trees gift us all three, and more besides. While trees act as the lungs of the Earth, taking in $CO_2$ and giving off huge quantities of oxygen, they also form an important rung of the water cycle, taking up water and giving it off to the skies that it might fall again as rain. They also hold water in the soil to prevent its dehydration and subsequent wind erosion, and suck up water that could cause flooding, whilst their leaf canopies mitigate the effect of heavy rainfall that could damage and erode soil. In human terms, entire civilisations are built on tree products, on timber for our homes, doors, floors, walls and windows, wooden cooking implements (and let us not forget the wood for fire itself, for cooking, protection and warmth), bowls, baskets, barrels, boxes and chests, furniture, carts, sledges, ploughs, ships, wheels, ladders and scaffolding, rubber, shoes, children's toys, pit props, paper, fabric, medicine, perfumes and incenses, mothballs, hair dye, chewing gum and even false teeth. Bog oak, ebony and other exotic woods are used for art and *objets d'art*. The discovery of charcoal and then of fossilised wood as coal enabled mankind to smelt metals and move on into the Iron Age and then the Industrial Age. We literally could not exist without them.

Sadly, just as humans exploit trees at the end of their lives, so they may exploit them as they are born: the practice of "greenwashing" (companies making often spurious claims to be greener than their competition) may include buying up farmland to plant acres of inappropriate tree species to decrease their carbon footprint. We are not sure this is entirely bad news, as the UK has the lowest density of tree cover in Europe – so every little helps!

While humans and animals have always eaten the fruits, nuts, seeds, the sap or syrup and even the leaves and shoots of trees (not to mention the spices derived from them, which include fruits, flowers, flower buds, roots and bark), many people may not realise that many of our medicines originated from them as well. Long before Boots the Chemist marketed aspirin, our ancestors had discovered the febrifuge and pain-killing qualities of willow bark; Australian aboriginals utilized eucalyptus (did you know this amazing tree often contains gold, which it takes up from the ground?) long before it was incorporated into modern common cold remedies. The bark of the cinchona tree (quinine) was used to treat malaria centuries ago – and it is still used today, though more often as a component of your gin and tonic! From ancient medicines to modern drugs and alternative therapies like Bach flower remedies, trees are healers – of people, of animals and of the planet.

There is an innate selflessness about trees: in the words of Sir Thomas Moore, "they say none harm, they think none harm, but wish everybody good." They take harmful substances from the air and consume them, giving forth life-giving oxygen; they mitigate pollution, and in return for the micronutrients they suck from the soil, they shed their leaves, gifting rich compost for the plant and animal organisms underneath. According to the Woodland Trust, a well-established oak tree can give off up to a quarter million litres of oxygen every year. Every tree is a wildlife sanctuary in itself, providing shelter, refuge, food, water, even a complete environment; for bats (which also use them for navigation), birds, monkeys and apes, sloths, tree frogs, squirrels, martens, possums, cats, bears and koalas, lizards and snakes, insects and other invertebrates; even parasitic plants that suck their nutrients are allowed to survive on their limbs; also mosses, lichens and fungi. A mature tree can play host to thousands of species, of which some will be *obligate*, that is, thriving only on this species of tree. Many pagans would also tell you that natural woods are the home of many spirits, including the Fae. That is not difficult to believe when you enter the peaceful paths of a wood and feel the changes it brings to your brainwave rhythms, your mood and your spirit.

One more subject that might occur to anyone who has had anything to do with roads, buildings and nearby trees is the sheer physical power of trees. It has been remarked that plant life has huge power: flimsy weeds can tear through tarmac and even concrete, and how much more so do trees, which can break nearby buildings, pipes, road surfaces and infrastructure, seemingly effortlessly, as they grow. These are puissant beings.

## THE "WOOD WIDE WEB"

Now we come to a subject which must strike the reader as pure magic, as it certainly did us. The character in the old movie *Paint Your Wagon* might talk to the trees, and they might or might not talk back, but *they certainly talk to one another!* While you might imagine trees would compete viciously with one another, as many animal species do, a forest is actually less a collection of individuals and more a community than we ever suspected: trees communicate with one another, make friends, warn one another of danger if they themselves are damaged, send nutrients to young saplings or to mature trees that are unwell. It is all very reminiscent of the Goddess-figure Eywa in the 2009 movie *Avatar*, who eventually sees off the bad human beings who have invaded her planet to abuse and despoil. We wonder whether our own trees and animals will ever turn on us like this for our ruthless exploitation of and damage to the Earth!

People have always felt in their water that there was more to a tree than a big stick of wood and some leaves. For beings without facial features or digits, trees are good at making themselves felt and understood, and there are plenty of stories in folklore about trees expressing their opinions, for example by fatally hurling a piece of timber at a landowner watching as his men cut them down on his orders. The phenomenon of tree hugging, which had its roots in historic peaceful protest against deforestation, has grown in popularity amongst spiritual people. In Wicca we are taught to approach trees with reverence and if we need a piece of their tissue for some reason, perhaps for a wand or some Ogham *fews*, to politely ask for it, giving something in return.

No one looks askance any longer at people who, like HRH Prince Charles, talk to their plants, and even the Royal Horticultural Society recommends this practice after carrying out a study of their own. They found clear evidence that plants and crops do respond to human speech, even that they prefer a female voice. Some gardeners play music in their greenhouses to encourage plants to thrive and bear fruit.

Whilst not approved by the scientific community at large, Cleve Backster's experiments with a polygraph device on plants in the 1960s started many people suspecting that there was more to green plants than a pretty face and if they were already in the habit of talking to their plants, they were possibly not surprised. Backster's experiments recorded pot plants responding to unfortunate shrimp being dropped into boiling water, to nearby plants being deliberately harmed and – more astonishing still – just to his own thoughts of damaging the plants by burning their leaves, which apparently produced a detectable effect on the polygraph record. Backster came to believe that all plants, and indeed all living organisms, were interconnected and capable of influencing one another. *Supernature* author, Dr Lyall Watson, who documented these results in his 1974 book, *The Romeo Error,* dubbed this concept the "Cosmic Mind". Watson carried out experiments of his own, involving recording the reactions of pot plants which "witnessed" another plant being deliberately damaged. He wrote that the "witnesses" were able to pick out the perpetrator from six people. However, in one case, the plants responded with fear to *two* of the researchers, including a participant who had not damaged a pot plant. Inquiries revealed that the person had been mowing his lawn that day! Watson also wrote of Native Americans whose custom it was to rush into the woods shouting threats at the trees before cutting down the chosen tree for a totem pole. This, they believed, had the effect of making all the trees "faint" – an anaesthetic for the one that was cut down.

From the 1990s, discoveries were beginning to be made about the importance of the mycorrhiza – the fungal net that runs under the ground in woodland areas and helps the trees to take up nutrients from the soil. Far from being an unimportant layer of organic matter, these fungal beings form a symbiotic relationship with the trees around whose roots they grow and which are vital to the trees' ability to feed from the soil, in the same way that humans need the beneficial bacteria in their gut in order to digest food. But the most fascinating thing about the mycorrhiza is that it *actually connects and allows trees to communicate with one another,* in the same way that people use the Internet.

Professor Suzanne Simard, a scientist based at the University of British Columbia's Department of Forest and Conservation Sciences, who made these discoveries, also put forward the theory of a "mother tree" – a hub around which all this mycorrhizal activity takes place. These mother trees are proactive in sending nutrients to their own saplings – just like animal mothers – they infect them with the necessary fungus, and also adapt their own roots to accommodate their offspring. And if this all sounds a bit like something from a Disney animation, it gets a bit more real with the information that there are bad guys in the mix as well: some trees quarrel, some plants hack into the system to steal nutrients, and some trees, notably the black knight ... sorry, er ... black walnut, may poison nearby trees that they see as rivals.

Whilst trees may "talk" to one another by means of this Wood Wide Web, they may also communicate in a more human way through sounds. While trees and woods are places filled with noise – from the wind in the branches, the creaking of boughs, birdsong and the sounds of arboreal animals and insects – trees themselves do produce sound. Scientists have been able to measure "plant bioacoustics" – the sound waves created by trees and plants, and which seem to have an effect on normal plant activities such as the growth of roots. The action of roots beneath the soil produces sounds, which can be sonic or ultrasonic, and these may be received by other plants nearby, who will respond to the messages that they carry. The sounds are within the range 10-240Hz, and the ultrasonic sound emissions are within 20-300kHz, and plants have been shown to respond to sounds within these ranges by growing towards the source of the vibrations. If you have very good hearing, try putting your ear against the ground near the base of a tree, or against its trunk, and see whether you can hear internal sounds that the tree produces. Tree frequencies can also be picked up by sensitive recording equipment or through a stethoscope held against the trunk.

Scientists also found that sounds emitted by non-plant sources, such as the buzzing of bees, could affect the plants: a species of Evening Primrose was found to rev up its nectar production and sweeten the quality of its nectar when it "heard" bees approaching, and other plants have been shown to be stimulated to release pollen ready for the visiting insects to carry away. Not such a surprise after the discovery that plants respond to the human voice and to music. Trees also respond to less positive visitors, increasing the tannin content of their leaves, to make them too bitter for caterpillars that are munching on them, and also transmit warnings to nearby trees to prepare themselves for invasion. They can even emit pheromones that draw ally predators – such as ladybirds, which prey on aphids and other pests – to their aid. Obviously, trees do not have physical brains, so they cannot have consciousness as we understand it, and yet ....

These discoveries point to the trees being well aware of non-plant beings traversing their territory; perhaps they know more about us than we do ourselves, when you consider that all people and animals give off pheromones and other chemical traces, and that trees may even be able to sense moods and auras. We would go a step further and suggest that trees, with their interconnectedness, are a vital part of what the Norsemen called the Web of Wyrd, of destiny and the universe as a body. Using the Ogham taps into this web in a very meaningful and magical way that, as mere humans, we cannot really understand.

In his 1998 book, *Magical Guardians*, Philip Heselton writes of trees as just that – as magical beings which exercise a protective and beneficial effect on the planet, which have spirit and even consciousness. With what we know in the twenty-first century, it is easy to think his writings did not go far enough, that there is far more to trees than we ever suspected, that they are even divinities, protective, benign and all-knowing. What insanity has led Man to damage and kill these beings, to cut them down for his selfish needs?

Within modern human lifetimes, trees have come under siege from tree plagues that have appeared and suddenly decimated tree populations: Dutch elm disease arrived in the UK in the 1960s, changing the face of the English countryside almost overnight, although it was known and named in 1921. In 2021 another pathogen, *Phytophthora pluvialis*, suddenly arrived in the UK in a Cornish woodland, where authorities immediately took steps to isolate it. Oak decline, ash blight and ash emerald borer beetle, horse chestnut canker … there are dozens of them (and rising) in the UK alone. This is on top of changing climate conditions which saw at least eight million trees felled in the UK by a succession of storms in the winter of 2021/2022; at the time of writing, the cost of storms Dudley, Eunice and Franklin in early 2022 had still not been calculated. Are the trees sick because of pollution and pollution-driven climate change or because of international travel and transportation of species, or is there a deeper reason? Do they know something we don't? Are trees leaving the planet?

# 3

# Connecting with Trees

The first remark that came to our minds when considering this subject was: why wouldn't you? Why wouldn't you want to connect with these awesome, benign and spiritual beings that give so much and take so little? The experience will not only teach and enrich you but may well bring you more benefits in the shape of reduced stress, improved health and wellbeing, and an uplifted spirit. You may even make a new friend!

The practice of tree hugging is often spoken of with a little sneer, typically by the spiritually unawakened, but particularly by rich property developers who care nothing for wildlife and are in the habit of ploughing into any green spaces they acquire and building profitable high-density housing developments on them. They can have little idea of the benefits of this old practice, which actually began in the early eighteenth century, when the inhabitants of an Indian village attempted to protect sacred trees which were to be cut down to build a palace. Although the villagers were murdered and the trees were cut down anyway, laws were later passed forbidding the felling of trees in villages inhabited by the strand of Hinduism to which the victims belonged. Modern times have seen activists embracing or even camping in the top branches of trees and chaining themselves to trees under threat of felling for motorways and new railway routes.

However, tree hugging does not have to take place purely as a reaction to some tree-threatening situation but can be enjoyed as a life-affirming action that nurtures the spirit, calms the mind and brings benefits to your physical health. If a walk in a beautiful wood can be seen as dessert after the labours of the day, then tree hugging is the cream on top.

If you would like to try tree hugging but do not have the faintest idea how to go about it, here are some simple suggestions. Connecting with trees is best done on their territory, i.e. the woods. Here there are many trees to choose from and you will be safer from prying eyes and able to express yourself without fear of being laughed at by ignorant people. However, you must also keep yourself safe, and it is advisable to go with your partner or a like-minded friend, someone who will ensure you are safe from harm; and take your mobile phone with you, and even a rape alarm. People can be a lot less pleasant than trees. If you do not have access to any woodland areas, try your local park – again with a friend for safety – or if you have trees in your garden, that is another possibility, and a much more safe and convenient one.

- Find your area: if you are lucky enough to live near a woodland area, make a habit of visiting it whenever you can, perhaps take your dog there. The more often you visit the trees, the more attuned you will become to their different vibrations, their personalities.

- Choose your tree. Don't just swagger up to the nearest trunk that is free from brambles and nettles: prepare yourself. Still your mind (which is very easy in woodland), stand for a while, or wander through the trees until a tree calls to you. You may have preconceptions about the tree you will choose (or which chooses you); perhaps you are drawn to a particular species that means a lot to you. That is fine, but do not close your mind to other trees, which may wish to connect. One will stand out, catch your attention; they are good at this. Some trees may discourage you from approaching them; perhaps they are suffering from a disease, or have endured damage at the hands of humans, or are just not in the mood that day.

Respect their feelings and concentrate on trees that have a welcoming vibe; you can always try those trees again another day. You may find that one tree becomes very special to you, and that you desire to return to this tree again and again – you have made a friend!

- Approach a tree. Go up to the tree which has made itself known, or that you feel you would like to connect with – assuming it has not refused your connection. Take your time and open your mind to the tree; there are several ways to embrace and connect.

- Move close to the tree slowly, as you would with an animal you did not wish to alarm. Give the tree a chance to check you out, feel your mood and your thoughts. Trees get enough humans coming by and slashing them with sticks, hacking initials into them or breaking their branches; give this tree the opportunity to see you are not one of those people. Ask it, either aloud or mentally, if it is happy to permit you this contact.

- Physically connect with the tree. The most obvious way is the classic hug, where you put your arms around the trunk, press your cheek to the tree and luxuriate in its feelings. If you find this posture uncomfortable and hard to maintain, try placing your palms before you against the tree and just leaning lightly into it. You can also place your cheek against the tree with this posture. If you plan to be there for an extended period, you can also simply sit on the ground with your back against the trunk, tipping your head back so it too rests against the trunk (this last position may cause you to fall asleep, lulled by the loving emanations of the tree!). It is important, as in meditation, to be comfortable, as otherwise you will be jiggling about and your mind will not be on the connection you are trying to make.

- Empty your mind of all thoughts and worries, which you may well find easier than you anticipated, as the tree's own vibrations will help. Open your mind to the tree, allowing any sensations or feelings it sends to enter your consciousness. Be aware of the physicality of the tree, of its roots going deep, deep into the ground, of the branches and twigs lifting high into the sky. Of the skin of the tree, coated in moss but still sensitive. Of each tiny twig touching the sky, of the surface of leaves and the sensations of moving sap. Let the tree see into your soul, let it see that you value it and mean it nothing but good. You may be astonished at what you get back, and it might not be a good idea to drive soon afterwards, in case your roots have difficulty with the pedals!

- When it is time to disconnect, say a farewell to the tree and explain that you have to go now. Then move away from the tree. You may feel moved to leave an offering for your new friend. In Wicca we leave small gifts for trees that have helped us, perhaps by allowing us to take pieces of their wood for magical purposes: small silver coins or a lock of our own hair. In Druidry it is the same: small gifts of natural material, not plastic, are left for the tree. But Wendy says, *my own feeling is that a bottle of water with some plant food in it might be a better gift for a tree.* It might also be a good idea to have something to eat and drink yourself, to ground you after your experience. Eat with the tree in comradeship, then scatter a few crumbs and pour a little of the drink at the base of the tree and bless it, saying any words that seem good to you, before leaving.

- It is a good idea to record your experiences as soon as you can in your journal or Book of Shadows, as later you may not recall every detail, and the notes you take will be a resource later on when you need inspiration. The one remark you will certainly make is that the tree has spirit, has consciousness, even if it is of a kind that is very different to your own.

Meditating under a tree is another fine way to connect, and choosing the same tree each time can bring considerable benefits. Perhaps you are lucky enough to have a beautiful tree in your garden, perhaps with a bench underneath, or a grassy space where you can sit. If your garden is very small, you could plant a very small tree in a pot and use this in the same way. The tree can become a very special sanctuary for you with time and can even shelter an outdoor altar and a place for offerings. Establishing a meditation habit (daily, if the weather permits) will have benefits for both of you, as the tree will enjoy the calm feelings you give off, and you will similarly benefit from the tree's energies, which will improve the quality of your meditation experience. Greet the tree as you pass it each day – even if you are not headed to your meditation place – and look after its health. Clear brambles and weeds away and perhaps spray the tree with natural remedies (such as water in which elder leaves have been stewed) if you find it has attracted pests. In the autumn, carefully fork in a little plant food around its roots and prune if necessary, explaining to the tree what you are doing and why.

More advanced practitioners may develop a "virtual" tree, grove or even an entire forest for meditation, in the same way some magical practitioners create and maintain a mental temple for work when their own place and tools are not available. The imagined environment is set up over the course of time, and may be based on a real place, in which case memory will aid the visualisation. This will take some imagination, but with much reinforcement over a prolonged period of time it can become very real and easy to conjure up when you need a special space but are perhaps away from home.

Tree hugging may present a few problems if you are mobility-challenged, but there are still ways in which you can connect with the trees, which will be aware of your difficulties and will certainly reach out to you in their own way if you make the first move. If you are unable to stand against a tree or even to get close enough to touch the trunk, try sitting for a while under the branches of the tree and opening your mind to it in the manner mentioned above. The mere presence of the tree will be enough to produce an effect on your mind, body and spirit, and you may well find that you experience much, if not all, that anyone might feel who is able to go up close and embrace the tree.

Ogham is another great way to connect with trees and the building of your set of Ogham is an opportunity to spend time on each species in the series. Create your Ogham set slowly by connecting to one tree at a time, making each *few* of the appropriate wood, but taking your time to connect with the tree and learn all you can about it, meditating near it and on it until you really feel a connection – *before* you ask for a twig to make your *few*. When, and only when, you have gone through this process with every tree in the Ogham alphabet, will you be ready to start your journey as an Ogham practitioner, using the *fews* for magic, healing and divination. For each *few*, you will need a piece of wood taken from the relevant tree, but the shape and size will depend on what kind of *fews* you want. The most traditional sets are in the form of small wands a few inches long, cut from a fairly narrow branch and with the bark removed from one half of the length, or just removed from a section along one side of the stave (keeping the bark on helps keep the identity of the wood). The Ogham symbol for that letter is then carved, burned or painted onto the stripped portion of the *few*, which can be varnished or oiled if you wish. Try to keep the *fews* the same length, though some may be a little gnarly, due to the habit of the tree they came from, and some, such as the reed, will look different from the others in any case (if you opt for other, non-woody plants specified for the *fews*, for example the wheatstraw for Ngetal, you could create the *few* by binding several heads of wheat or stalks of a plant together in a tight bundle. It will not be possible to paint or burn the Ogham symbol onto this bundle, but its own appearance will identify it sufficiently). Some people like to cut small blocks, dice or rounds from the wood instead, to create Ogham *fews* in the same way as Norse runes, and these can look very fine, though the visual identity of the tree will be lost when you shape the *fews*, and some of the trees do not lend themselves to this idea, again notably the reed. Sandie knows at least one Druid who does not use wood at all for his sets, but will choose pebbles, shells, ceramic tiles or whatever is available, and paint the symbols on them. One final word on making your *fews*: you will need to ensure that letters that could be mistaken for one another – like Beith (birch) and Uath (hawthorn), Luis (rowan) and Duir (oak) – are clearly marked so you know which way up they are meant to be. Beith has one *flesc* (horizontal stroke) on the right of the ridge and Uath has one on the left; Luis has two strokes on the right and Duir has two on the left, and so on – easy to confuse if you're not sure which way up they are. We suggest giving the base ridge its triangular base but not repeating the shape at the top, as with written Ogham; or simply drawing a line under the base of the letter, as you sometimes see on handwritten tickets to differentiate the numerals 6 and 9.

Making each *few* will take time – and should – as you learn to know the tree, then make the physical stave. You should then carry the *few* with you for a while to allow yourself to receive any messages and impressions it may have for you, and also open your eyes to any signs it may give – you may, for example, see the Ogham symbol in nature, in clouds, in the fire or in other ways such as street signs, advertisements, or in the backgrounds of TV programmes. This is the same way in which rune practitioners train their minds to be open to receive messages from the runes.

Having got this far in your study of Ogham and the trees, we imagine you will feel an increased desire to look after the wellbeing of trees on our beleaguered planet, where forest acres fall daily to the selfish desires of man … to his own ultimate detriment. We pagans like to think we aren't quite as bad as some of these exploiters of Nature, and many of us give back as much as we can and live as sustainably as we can, whether that means eschewing a car and never travelling by air, or just using eco-friendly washing-up liquid and recycling food packaging.

Fighting for trees can be done on a very small scale – not everyone owns a large estate that can be rewilded. A small, terraced house can be the centre of some very interesting ideas to help the ecology, from the way the small garden is planted to forays to take part in guerrilla gardening on verges and weedy spaces nearby! Of course, if you do have your own land, or even a larger garden, you can proactively plant native trees and encourage wildlife by building ponds and leaving places for nettles and other caterpillar foods to thrive. You could even plant your own grove for Druid rituals. If your garden has specimens that do not help the environment, such as Leylandii, which suck all goodness from the soil for some distance around them, consider replacing them with broadleaf trees and shrubs.

Even in death we can help trees. If you are of an age to be considering a funeral plan, why not think about woodland burial? Since 1993, when the first natural burial site was opened in Carlisle, woodland burial sites have been springing up all over the UK, with families choosing natural biodegradable materials for coffins, such as wicker and cardboard, and even more unusual substances such as banana leaf, seagrass and wool. The grave may then be marked by the planting of a sapling rather than a traditional headstone, comforting the bereaved family and friends with the knowledge that the site will continue to grow and one day become beautiful natural woodland of which their loved one is a part. The venue is certainly rather less depressing than standing in a traditional graveyard on a rainy day watching a coffin being lowered into the ground – why does it always rain at interments?

Support an organisation like the Woodland Trust, which cares for woodlands and actively plants trees; or Earthwatch, which plants forests across the world and currently has a "Tiny Forest" scheme to plant small but dense woodlands in the UK. You can sponsor trees through these organisations, give them as gifts or even buy your own and plant them on your land. The Order of Bards, Ovates and Druids (OBOD) has had a tree- and grove-planting scheme since 1988 – the year after the hurricane in the UK that cost us so many trees – offering support and advice to anyone wanting to plant trees. Their members have planted thousands of trees and many groves across the world. Or you could even become militant and protest against the cutting down of trees in your town or area. Get your green hat on!

# 4

# The Healing of Trees

With typical Eastern acceptance of Nature's mystical properties, the Japanese have combined their love of trees with hard-headed business sense in a practice that might leave Western office managers scratching their heads. Tired and stressed Japanese executives are often ordered to take time off for therapy – not to the medical centre, but to the nearest woodland area. "Forest bathing", as it is known, or the Japanese practice of *shinrin-yoku*, is known to lower blood pressure, cut down the likelihood of heart attacks, strokes and even cancer, and reduce anxiety, stress and depression. This is something everyone can experience for themselves by simply walking through woodland and noticing how the very presence of the trees seems to soothe away stress, reduce anxiety and fill the mind and body with tranquillity (this effect of trees is so powerful that it can even be felt around dead wood: in a furniture warehouse where wooden chests, tables and chairs surround you, astonishingly, some of the same effects can be experienced). Of course, the trees are not the only therapy on offer: the patients also experience massage, meditation, healthy food and are led into an all-encompassing mindfulness in which they empty their minds of anything but sensory experiences such as smelling trees and flowers, seeing the beauty of nature, walking on small smooth stones and hearing birdsong. While this all sounds a bit fanciful to Westerners, research has shown that there is at least one scientific basis for the healing that people experience: volatile organic substances called phytoncides are released by trees and plants, which can boost the human immune system and fight infection.

Shinrin-yoku already has its adherents in the West, notably HRH the Duchess of Cambridge, who in 2019 helped design an entry based on shinrin-yoku for the Chelsea Flower Show. Forestry England has already shown they are open to the idea and advice can be found on their website for getting the most out of the practice, including walking slowly through the forest areas, turning off all phones and IT devices, being aware of sensory experiences around you and taking deep, relaxing breaths as you go.

Now the National Health Service has twigged that this might be a low-cost way of helping British residents and in 2020 a £4 million budget was announced for "Green Social Prescribing" – a long-term plan to treat physical and mental health through community projects involving nature and plants. This can be as simple as taking country walks or could involve gardening or wildlife conservation schemes, and the move could be a first step towards UK doctors prescribing forest bathing for their patients.

The Japanese are still researching and discovering the benefits of trees: in 2004 a study demonstrated that not only did a walk in the woods lower blood pressure and benefit the heart and immune system, but people who just looked at a wooded view for 20 minutes had a measurable 13 per cent drop in their levels of cortisol, the stress hormone.

Other countries have realised that the mere presence of trees has a natural healing ability and have taken steps to utilise this in many ways. In New York, the iconic Mount Sinai Hospital was redesigned so that wards faced onto Central Park, so that the view of treetops and greenery might boost recovery. Other places have taken note of the effect, with the result that the ground-breaking Milanese "highrise forests" project, Bosco Verticale, has won not only universal praise from architects and townscapers, but also the International Highrise Award. These two towers, 111 metres and 76 metres high and completed in 2014, provide a habitat for more than 900 trees, plus shrubs and groundcover plants between them and may eventually be emulated across the world.

Since 2014, the Birmingham Forest Research Facility (BIFoR) has also been studying trees for their healing abilities – in this case, their ability to heal themselves and combat global warming. The project uses six rings of towers built into mature woodland with non-invasive construction and incorporating various devices for measuring trees' responses. Under the eye of a consortium of top scientists, researchers conduct experiments such as pumping pure carbon dioxide onto the tree canopies, to measure how well the trees might react to increasing levels of carbon pollution. They are also researching into the trees' ability to defend themselves from some of the tree plagues and pests that have ravaged the globe in recent years.

Trees have always healed people. Long before forest bathing (which became popular in Japan in the 1980s), mankind had aspirin, quinine, morphine, eucalyptus and many other tree- and plant-derived remedies. Even just in the UK, trees make up a pharmacopeia to rival the counter at Boots, with some trees having always been grown near cottages and farmsteads for their healing properties as well as their beauty.

Elder (*Sambucus nigra*) is a prime example with its bark, flowers and berries all carrying healing chemicals. Wendy recounts that when she had young children, she used to make up a syrup every autumn by heating the berries gently in the oven until they popped, then pressing and straining them before adding 1lb (450g) of sugar and a clove or two to each pint (500ml) of juice. This was boiled for a few minutes to produce a thickened syrup, which was then bottled. A teaspoon of this can stop a cold in its tracks, soothe sore throats and ease coughs. Elder bark tea will break a fever and stop a headache and cure the aching that often comes with flu and colds. The flowers make a tea which has the same effects as the fruit, but also acts as a diuretic. This tisane can be frozen in ice cube trays for future use (it is also an amazing skin tonic).

Apples (one a day keeps the doctor away!) help the gut: the fruit acts as a laxative but, oddly, grated apple can also ease diarrhoea, as can the bark. Apple cider and cider vinegar have many health-giving properties and the latter has become a favourite health drink as a result, with claimed benefits including lowered blood sugar, better hair condition, stronger nails, weight loss and improvements to heart health and the digestive system. Many tree- and shrub-based food additives carry both health-enhancing properties and good flavours which have caused them to become an integral part of a culture's cuisine, and it is hard to say which came first. Tea, which is the second most popular drink in the world after water, was probably originally brewed in China as a medicine or tonic, and only later became popular as a stimulant and refreshing drink. The seeds of the cacao tree, originally discovered by the Mayans and used in religious ritual, are now the basis of an immense industry covering confectionery of all kinds, baked products and drinks, with chocolate having become closely associated with Christian and other religious festivals. Whilst it has admittedly become a food associated with overindulgence and unhealthy eating, chocolate is actually packed with micronutrients and chemicals that can promote bodily health and fill the brain with alertness and a sense of well-being due to its serotonin content: there's a reason why someone whose relationship has ended often chooses to binge on chocolate!

There has been a huge interest in recent times in the product called pau d-arco, made from the very ornamental trees of the South American Tabebuia species, sometimes called the roble tree. Pau d'arco bark is an herbal treatment taken as a tea, which could help a number of conditions, from thrush to cancer. Pau d'arco is also often added to the ayahuasca drug taken for spiritual reasons.

Across the world, people are really only scratching the surface of the chemical healing properties of trees, and it has been suggested that many vital healing plants may already have been lost with the destruction of the Amazon rainforests.

## CELTIC REIKI

Reiki is a Japanese healing and magical art introduced by Dr Mikao Usui (1865-1926), a student of medicine, theology and psychology who discovered the effect while fasting and praying for three weeks – under a sacred tree! – on the top of Mount Kurama, near Kyoto. Dr Usui believed that all creatures have the innate ability to heal themselves, or even others, using a power that comes from the universe and flows through the healer – so that he or she is not depleted or left exhausted or unwell by delivering this healing to another. Reiki can be safely used on oneself, on others, on animals and plants and can even be sent to someone far away or used to ameliorate a situation, such as a quarrel between two people or a period of misfortune. It can be used on greater issues, such as the health of the planet or strife between countries. It involves laying hands either on the patient or above them (in the case of individuals who do not feel comfortable with being touched) while letting the power flow through for a period of time, perhaps an hour or less. Those experiencing the healing may report a feeling of extreme heat in the place where the practitioner's hands are placed, and afterwards report that this was the start of a real improvement in their condition. Practitioners will tell you that even a few minutes of Reiki will deliver some help to a person feeling stressed or unwell when there is not sufficient time for a full healing session.

Reiki as a practice is taught to students in two or three stages, along with a series of symbols which are used to awaken and concentrate the healing effect. The students then receive an attunement to start their ability to channel Reiki healing. Wendy uses Reiki, but as she has never felt comfortable with or aligned to the Japanese symbols, which are culturally alien to her, she has always used a simple pagan pentagram.

Similarly, Celtic Reiki uses symbols taken from the Ogham to invoke the healing power of the trees, or their power for other purposes, such as raising power for magic and luck. To a British person, they start out with an advantage over the Japanese Reiki system, as the trees, their familiarity in our landscapes, their stories and folklore and their place in our culture reach out to us in a way that a practice and its associated symbology from another culture could not.

Celtic Reiki is taught in the same way as the Japanese practice, with a period of study followed by attunements. The system was developed in the 1990s by British author and lifestyle therapist, Martyn Pentecost, who discovered the healing energies of a tree in a Welsh graveyard, ironically, while trying to heal the tree: he was giving Usui Reiki to it because it was dying after being damaged by lightning. (He recounts an experience of feeling the tree's energies while placing his hand between the stump and the fallen portion of the tree, which recalls the ancient practice of passing a sick person through a gap or hole in a tree to heal them). Pentecost went on to work with a range of trees and shrubs – especially those which he knew the ancient Druids had held in esteem – and went on to develop a system tied to the Ogham alphabet, using the Ogham *fews* as symbols to initiate the healing energy.

Practitioners choose the Ogham symbols to use based on the meaning of the associated trees so that, for example, a person suffering from stagnation and an inability to move on might be treated with the Idad symbol, which will bring the regenerative energies of yew into the equation; and a person dreading change and new situations might be benefited by Beith, birch. For healing of more physical ailments, the practitioner might call on the energies of healing trees in a holistic way, spending an hour or more focusing energies into the person until they have achieved a deep state of relaxation in which healing can be manifested. As with Usui Reiki, the power does not come from the practitioner, but is drawn up from the earth, so that the person doing the healing is not drained or weakened by a loss of their personal energy. The system is based on the alternative Beith-Luis-Nion order of the *fews*, and the Reiki energy healing may be supplemented by herbal remedies made from the healing trees and plants. Practitioners also make use of the *correspondences* of the *fews*, the colours, crystals and other items magically associated with them. The system has grown and expanded and practitioners may now use chakras, crystals, pathworkings and other elements to implement the tree- and plant-based Celtic Reiki healing.

Celtic Reiki can be used in a similar way for magic and spiritual development, again using the symbols of the Ogham letters to bring the energy of a particular tree or trees into whatever work is being done, as well as visualisations and even the use of physical matter from the trees and plants, perhaps burned as incense or used as a smudge to cleanse and activate the room before the working begins, or simply present on the altar to bring the presence of the tree into the working. When you consider that the presence of a living tree or plant brings its energies perceptibly into the space it occupies, and that this effect may even be felt in the presence of timber that has been cut down and made into furniture, as we noted above, you will understand how powerful the addition of this material could be to any kind of magical or spiritual work.

# 5

# Using Tree Ogham for Divination and Magic

Human beings know everything. And before you start thinking this is a snide comment on the arrogance of our species, it isn't. Because we are part of the Ancient Ones, we may potentially know everything that they do. Innately, we have all knowledge, but it is blocked off from us by our preconceptions, by our upbringing, by our prejudices, by our lack of belief and spiritual insight, by our mortality and our position within time. This is why, pagans believe, using a pendulum works, using Tarot cards works, using runes, Ogham staves, a scrying bowl or a saucer of tea leaves works. These items act as a catalyst or conduit for our own ability to sense what is going on, powered by our belief in them, their importance to us as magical tools, their *specialness*. This is how all magical tools work, not just the implements of divination. In and of themselves, they are pieces of wood, of ceramic, of glass, of metal … it is the power in us that makes the magic and these items serve merely to conjure forth this power.

Anyone who is drawn to the Ogham will find it works for them: it's a kind of non-vicious circle. It is magical because you believe it is magical; without this feeling – which is hard to explain to someone who does not practise magic or divination – this special regard for, this *joy* in the object, it will not work for you. This can almost be likened to sex: sex does not work unless you have this attraction, this urge, this special feeling.

Part of the magic attaching to the tools you use comes from your own involvement in physically creating them. Of course, there are tools you have inherited or bought or found ready-made that you have done nothing to except a cleansing and consecration (Tarot cards, for example, cannot easily be created from scratch) but you may well have found that the things you have made yourself have much more bang for your buck, more *zing* than those you bought in that little shop in the High Street. And of those you acquired rather than made, the ones you have personalised, perhaps by scratching your personal bindrune into them or decorating them with beads and crystals, or in some other way embellishing them, have more power than the unvarnished shop-bought items.

The foregoing advertisement is just Wendy's usual spiel to her students, but it is important, and now that you have made your own Ogham set – which may have taken you many months – you will certainly agree about the special feeling you get from it because you have made it yourself.

If you find using or making the *fews* difficult for any reason, you can buy them as cards. The chief of the British Druid Order, Philip Shallcrass (also known by his Druid name of Greywolf) designed a set of Ogham oracle cards which a lot of people find much simpler to use for divination rather than the *fews*, and other sets are also available.

## OGHAM AS AN ORACLE

Ogham is harder to learn than the Tarot and the runes, for the divinatory meanings of the *fews* are often vague and not universally agreed upon and it could be said there are as many meanings as there are practitioners. This was the bad news. The good news is that you can and will learn to use the Ogham as a very personal oracle, if you first work at getting to know them and allowing them to teach you their meanings *for you*. Anyone who uses the tarot or the runes will tell you they develop a special relationship with the oracle, which will then deliver messages that are not standard given meanings, but personal to the user. This phenomenon will be recognised by anyone who uses magic or divination as part of their spiritual life. Start your journey with the Ogham by making notes (in a book or on a computer) on each of the letters as they speak to you. Whilst you should certainly learn the given meanings of the *fews*, the special meaning they have for you is important. Perhaps you had a big apple tree in your family's garden when you were little, where you went to read when you wanted to be alone, or a friendly elder tree that seemed to comfort you when you were down. Maybe there was a hawthorn that you raided for twigs and thorns to make "pens" or catapults, or a gloomy yew tree that stood at the gate of the school where you were unhappy and bullied. These experiences and memories will colour the messages the trees have for you, even though they are not part of the canonical meanings of the trees.

Each Ogham *few* will have many layers of meaning, largely but not exclusively based on the history of its tree and that tree's nature and qualities, its relationship with mankind and its place in tradition and popular culture. Each tree is also associated with colours, animals, birds, plants and planets and, in fact, has its own set of correspondences and the information associated with these. Modern Druids who use the Ogham regard it as a mystic map of the universe, in the same way rune scholars see their runes and Tarot readers their cards.

Treat your Ogham set as you would any magical tool: with respect and love. Keep them safe and clean and never use them frivolously or to show off. Carry them with you as often as you can, particularly when you first acquire or make them, so they become attuned to your personal energies and thoughts. In the long term, keep them somewhere special to you, such as under your altar or next to your bed.

It is a very good idea to meditate with your Ogham, in the same way as you might with runes or Tarot cards, in order to get to know them better. Sandie recalls that when she was new to Druidry and the Ogham she approached the *fews* with a pathworking of her own which simply came to her, *gathering the vowels in a bag and then climbing the "ladder" formed by the flescs on the main ridge with the bag on her shoulder*. This kind of visualisation can be very helpful in learning the *fews* and in opening your mind and spirit to their messages.

Deploying the Ogham is done in exactly the same way as the runes: they can be drawn one at a time from their bag or drawn as a handful and laid out, or just cast from the hands or from their bag to see which land uppermost, which lie side-by-side or across one another and which lie reversed. You yourself must decide in which direction they are read: whether you take the centre of the spread as the starting point or view the *fews* according to which compass points they are facing or spread them out one by one in a long line. It is even possible to use some of the traditional Tarot layouts, such as, rather appropriately, the Celtic Cross, in which each position on the layout represents an aspect of your life, such as health, career, love-life, and so on. One *few* may be drawn for a quick bit of guidance, or one of the simplest layouts is a row of three, in which the first one laid down represents the past leading to the current situation, the second or middle one represents the situation and the third suggests the outcome. Bear in mind that the staves will influence one another, especially those that fall side by side or even on top of each other: a *few* of bad omen which lies next to one of good meaning will not be so severe as you might have feared, and the *fews* might also suggest the areas of your life for which their messages are intended by this method.

If you have opted for tile-shaped Ogham *fews*, some letters may fall face down, their symbol on the underside; these are not read. Even the wand-shaped *fews* can fall in this way if they have been painted or engraved on one side only. This is something you must take into account from the outset, as if you are taking stock of all the staves, regardless of how they lie; you might consider drawing only a few – or you will get the same overall result every time! Some will fall facing away from you and this is called "reversed". Not all Ogham readers take notice of reversal, which can change the meaning of the letter significantly, but others do, and this is something you must decide for yourself at the outset, along with other quite basic decisions: do you acknowledge reversed *fews*? What exactly do you consider a reversal? Will this mean a letter that faces away from you by 180 degrees, or one that lies sideways-on to you? Don't go and get totally obsessed with this idea and dig out your old school protractor, but you should have an idea in your head as to what constitutes reversal.

Your frame of mind is also important. Never use your Ogham frivolously and if you don't like the answer you get, never toss the letters back in the bag and draw again: that is disrespectful and shows that you do not understand the nature of the oracle. Take time to clear your mind and adopt a respectful and receptive mood before you draw the Ogham. Ask your question carefully and when you have seen the answer, let it mull over in your mind, as the full meaning may not be clear straightaway. It may take a day or two for the full meaning to take shape in your mind, so write down what you have drawn and think about it.

When you are better acquainted with your set, you will start to notice the symbols in other ways – in clouds and hedgerows and spiders' webs, in manmade artefacts, and of course finding a leaf stuck on your shoulder or in your shoe may well be a message from the Ogham associated with the tree that dropped it.

The Ogham can be cast on a table or on the ground, or you could make or acquire a cloth upon which to cast them, either plain white or embroidered with symbols that mean something to you. Fabrics can be bought in so many patterns now, including sea waves, ripe corn and fields of flowers, that it should be easy enough to buy a print featuring trees or leaves, if that appeals to you. With a little care and ingenuity and a few fasteners, the casting cloth can be made into a bag to house the letters, unfolding into a flat sheet when needed. Some practitioners may prefer a board on which to cast; again, this can be made as plain or as embellished as you wish.

## OGHAM AND TREES FOR MAGIC

Wood has been a sacred material for mankind for thousands of years, from the wood henges created by our ancestors (like the timber circle recently discovered in East Yorkshire) to the wood used by modern pagans to make wands, wand-athames, staffs, stangs, pentacles, lamens, pendants, altars and magical boards, runes and the chests used for storing magical items.

Wood is also seen as inherently magical when it is part of the home: the two areas of the home considered most magical are the threshold and the hearth – which would once have burned nothing but wood – and an ancient protection attaches to doors, boundaries, fences and gates, especially those made of wood (and especially those with huge hobnails hammered into them, as iron is also seen as magically protective). Evil cannot enter the home unless it is invited – remember those old Dracula movies? When you come to look at the final section of this book, the Ogham letters themselves, you will notice that all of them include protection as one of their meanings. Trees are naturally protective, whether they are sheltering you from a storm when they are alive or sheltering you by forming the structure of your house and roof when they are dead, so it is obvious that they are protective magically as well.

Why is wood seen as so magical? Once it would have been pretty well the only material available for making magical items, but it is still the preferred choice and many practitioners will not use any modern, manmade material – plastic is especially disdained. Materials which were once part of living things are prized by witches, magicians and shamans, from bones and skins to seashells and of course wood – these being seen not only as gifts from nature but also as bringing with them the powers and qualities of the beings from which they originated. Trees are full of life, and there are plenty of accounts of dead sticks being thrust into the ground (as in the story of the Glastonbury Thorn) and later surprising the traveller by putting out green shoots and growing into a living tree. As we have seen, the trees themselves have powerful energies; a magical presence which they bring into any situation where they are used or called upon.

After the timber used to make an altar, the most obvious use of trees and plants is to decorate the sacred space for rituals. Most witches include flowers or greenery on the altar as part of a ritual, and plant material is traditionally used to garnish the altar or even the whole room at the eight pagan festivals, from the May blossoms used at Beltane to the Yule decorations of holly and other evergreens. Diane, a green witch, always brings a posy of carefully chosen magical herbs and flowers (which she grows in her garden) to a ritual. As you will see in the section on the Ogham themselves, they are all associated with different festivals, or Sabbats.

Wands, of which magical practitioners may have a whole array, may be fashioned from the wood of a carefully chosen tree to invoke a certain deity or spirit, or to perform certain kinds of magic. Some practitioners will prefer a wand made from a wood associated with their astrological birth sign or rising sign, or the planet with which they feel aligned. Druids will probably normally use an ash wand, as this tree is considered the basic magical wood. But for some purposes, a tree may be chosen for its correspondences; for example, a wand of birch may be used for magic to help a new project, or even in a spell to help a woman conceive a baby. A wand of rowan might be used for magical protection against a curse or evil spirits. A wand of apple would be useful in healing or love magic, and one of hazel for acquiring wisdom and inspiration.

The Ogham symbols themselves can be used in magic and ritual in the same way that the Tarot and the runes can be – placed on the altar and used for the focus of the magic or to draw certain energies into the sacred space. Idad, the yew, can be used in a Samhain ritual to honour the dead, while Muin, the vine, could be used to celebrate at Lughnasadh (the first harvest) or at Alban Elfed/Mabon (the second harvest), or at any ritual of thanksgiving for something achieved. Sandie advises that the Ogham sigils to be used for magic can be drawn onto bark left over from creating the *few* for the main set of Ogham, then hidden in places or burnt with other herbs in cleansing or banishing spells.

In the same way, the symbols can be inscribed on objects and used as charms, talismans or amulets (the difference between these three is that an amulet averts ill luck and danger, whilst charms and talismans attract good luck, in the case of the talisman for a specific purpose, such as in sports or business). The Quert (apple) symbol, for example, might be carried to a medical appointment if the wearer is worried about the diagnosis, and the Coll (hazel) symbol might be carried into an exam for inspiration. Fearn (alder) might be carried if you need a friend or some advice, and Nion (ash) if you need to stand up for yourself in a difficult situation in which your ethics or your beliefs are challenged.

In Druid magic, which is rather more earth-oriented than Wiccan magic, the *fews* themselves would be created with a closer regard for their own natural energies. While a witch might cut wood for a magical tool in the right moon phase for her purpose (such as, for example, when the Moon is full in Cancer for a home protection spell), a Druid would include considerations like the growing or fruiting season of the tree being used. Sandie explains that a piece of wood for a magical purpose cut from a tree that was dormant might bring "tired" energies into the working instead of dynamic ones. Because of a need to maximise the special energies of the Ogham in this way, a Druid and possibly a witch might create a separate Ogham *few* rather than using one from his or her own set. In any case, some witches will afterwards destroy items created especially for a spell, such as written incantations, poppets and talismans, which would leave your set minus a *few* every time you used it!

# 6

# Robert Graves and the Tree Calendar

Now we come to a subject that has caused controversy since its publication more than 70 years ago: the Ogham Tree Calendar. Some modern (and better informed) pagans will get quite warm under the collar about this concept, but in the interests of exploring the subject as fully as possible, we thought it best to include a section on it, if only to avoid elephant-in-the-room syndrome. Graves's book, *The White Goddess*, which has never been out of print since its publication in 1948, has been both a source of inspiration and of difference of opinion for modern pagans. We say: read it with an educated yet open mind – paganism is nothing if not eclectic and accepting of others' wisdom, provided that the source of that wisdom is clearly identified and no one is led to believe that a new idea is actually an ancient, traditional one.

This troubled writer (who as a young man declared himself an atheist) was very obviously enraptured with the Goddess by the time he wrote this study ... his very grave is sited on Mallorca, at a shrine once sacred to the Moon Goddess. The book is focused on the idea that Goddess worship was universal and times were better under this culture than under the Christian regime that followed and eradicated it. Reading the lush narrative in *The White Goddess* gives a clear sense of the author's spiritual engagement with his theme, as opposed to those of the popular cash-cows like *I, Claudius* and *Count Belisarius* which he wrote to earn a living.

Graves (1895–1985) was a poet, First World War soldier and sexual adventurer who followed his father, the Irish folklorist and poet, Alfred Graves, in being fascinated by Irish mythology. He became absorbed in the idea of Ogham and its history and with the cryptic ballad *Cad Goddeu* (Battle of the Trees), which appears to name the tree-*fews* one by one and even give information about them which could aid in their use as a divination tool; as well as with the ancient ballad called *The Song of Amergin*. Basing his ideas on material previously written by the seventeenth-eighteenth century historian, Roderic O'Flaherty, he divided up the year into thirteen months, adding an extra intercalary day to keep the calendar correct to the solar year. He used the Beith-Luis-Nion order of the Ogham but did not use all the symbols.

However, there are one or two problems with Graves's ideas. To begin with, the Celts had a perfectly useful calendar of their own based on lunar and solar rhythms, which gives us the fire festivals such as Samhain and Beltane (which are still celebrated today, even by non-pagans, as Halloween and May Day). An example of this calendar was found at Coligny in eastern France and is currently on display in the Palais des Arts Museum in Lyon. The bronze tablet, originally some 1.48 metres in length but broken into fragments of which 72 pieces survive, dates from the second century CE and shows a calendar based on twelve months with resonating names like *Giamonios* and *Aidrinios*, each month consisting of six five-day weeks. A second similar but much less complete calendar was found a few miles away. The Coligny calendar gives precedence to the lunar cycles, with each month representing a full lunation, and the total days are then rounded up carefully over a five-year cycle to reconcile the calendar with the solar year. Each month's name is based on its description, such as "summer", "cold", "winter" or "non-travelling". There is no historical proof whatsoever for a tree calendar like Graves's idea.

Graves also took liberties with the material; he tweaked the tree letters, choosing thirteen trees from the basic list of 20 and ignoring others, stating as his reason that some of these were "later forms". So, he omitted two of the consonant trees for some reason: Quert (apple), an important and sacred tree to the Celts; and Straif (blackthorn); as well as the vowel trees, which include the yew, another important tree for the Celts. His calendar, though apparently lunar, is anchored to Gregorian dates, with the months starting at the same time each year, regardless of the current moon cycle, and in fact his months are 28 days long, which corresponds neither with the full cycle of the Moon (29.5 days), nor with her orbit around the Earth (27.3), so that the calendar must very soon fall out of rhythm with the Moon, and also with the solar year, unless extra intercalary days are added at intervals. He even ignored astrological markers like the solstices and equinoxes. Graves also re-wrote parts of the *Song of Amergin* to fit with his theories and even invented his own "Celtic" tree Goddess, Druantia, who has since become very popular with modern pagans.

Many pagans took to the Tree Calendar with whoops of delight and it certainly is a very beautiful idea, as long as it is considered to be nothing more than a twentieth century concept which has no basis in historical fact. The idea then spawned both an array of books and websites, and tree astrology, in which birth signs become the Ogham letters Graves chose for each month, instead of the classical zodiac symbols. Again, an attractive idea, but one with no basis in ancient Celtic tradition.

The other small beef we have with the concept is that trees are present all year round; it is next to impossible to allocate a tree for each month, as trees live and grow in every month, they tend to blossom and fruit roughly around the same time, and drop their leaves at almost the same time in the autumn, and the only real difference to be remarked upon in the year is in the behaviours of deciduous and evergreen trees. Some trees do admittedly have a relationship with certain festivals, notably the Christmas tree, the Norwegian spruce, in Christian culture and the hawthorn in

## GRAVES' TREE CALENDAR

| | |
|---|---|
| 24th December to 20th January: | Beith |
| 21st January to 17th February: | Luis |
| 18th February to 17th March: | Nion |
| 18th March to 14th April: | Fearn |
| 15th April to 12th May: | Saille |
| 13th May to 9th June: | Uath |
| 10th June to 7th July: | Duir |
| 8th July to 4th August: | Tinne |
| 5th August to 1st September: | Coll |
| 2nd September to 29th September: | Muin |
| 30th September to 27th October: | Gort |
| 28th October to 23rd November: | Ngetal |
| 24th November to 22nd December: | Ruis |
| 23rd December: intercalary day | |

pagan belief (though Graves puts it in a month later than Beltane, with which pagans associate it), but to slot a tree into a whole lunation on account of this seems very arbitrary and artificial.

Because trees have a regular cycle which differs little from species to species, Graves has assigned some trees to times of the year with which they seem to have very little relevance. What is Beith (birch) doing at Christmas? It neither blossoms, fruits nor bears leaves at this time, nor does it have any obvious cultural ties to midwinter. Luis (rowan) is similarly dormant in January and February, producing its new leaves from March onwards. Similarly, he places the evergreen Tinne (holly) in the hottest part of summer, when its only cyclical difference to the other trees is that it keeps its leaves and its bright berries for the winter, so that it might have been a better match for the position occupied by Beith. This might have been more understandable if he had allocated Tinne to the month which covers midsummer, which in pagan tradition is when the Holly King defeats the Oak King and takes his throne – a metaphor for the passing of the highest point of the summer.

Another problem with the calendar is one that is inherent in the Ogham itself: it is decidedly British. No pagan living in Australia or South Africa, for example, will be able to relate to the tree-signs, as in most cases they will not know the trees Graves chose.

It is evident from online posts, artwork and blogs that many pagans are unaware of the artificial and modern origins of the Tree Calendar, and have come to accept it as of an importance approaching that of the Ogham themselves. Perhaps seduced by the attractions of the concept, they have not realised the importance of researching its pedigree, which is understandable: how much nicer and more appealing it is to be considered a beautiful birch tree instead of a goat!

# 7

# The Ogham

Now it is time to meet the stars of the show: the Ogham *fews* (letters) and pair them with their soulmates: the trees. We will meet each pairing of *few* and tree individually, and find out about its deeper meanings and its place within world mythology, folk lore, divination, magic and healing. Do not forget that the traditional uses of trees in the non-magical world creates magical meaning as well; for example, a tree used to make coffins might carry an ominous note, or a tree used to make sporting equipment might point towards a sporting victory. The letters also have links to other living things, as well as their own tree, animals and plants, and these can also be used as symbols or plant matter in magic and ritual involving each letter. For those who have worked with runes, we will include alignments with the runic alphabet where they occur (although they do not always match up) and with the Tarot and Qabalah. Each section concludes with a short visualisation or pathworking to help you really immerse yourself in the *few* and learn to know its "flavour".

The order of the Ogham can be seen as a life story: the series starts with birth, followed by protection (as in the protection your family gives you when you are a child), goes through the experiences of life, and finally reaches death – the last *few*. Protection is a common theme throughout the Ogham alphabet: all the trees are protective, but each has its own form of protection to offer, whether this is against ill-health, ill-fortune or evil magic. Another common theme with all the letters is the potential for transformation or transition: this opens up the magical use of the Ogham *fews* considerably, with practitioners having the ability to choose appropriate *fews* for work for both protection and transformation.

How do you pronounce Ogham? This can vary according to region and spelling – it is sometimes spelled Ogam, and can be pronounced O-wam or even Ohm. The next sections include pronunciation of the letter names and other information as well, including magical and astrological correspondences.

One further note: the letters have been associated with Sabbats, the eight ancient pagan festivals spread through the year, which may not be familiar to all our readers. Here is a table of the Sabbats and what they mean to pagans, which may be helpful when you read the information on the *fews*. This table is based on the Northern Hemisphere; if you live in the Southern Hemisphere the dates may be different; for example, the spring and autumn equinoxes and the two solstices will change places!

| Druid Name | Wiccan Name | Date | Meaning |
| --- | --- | --- | --- |
| Alban Arthan | Yule | The winter solstice, around 21st December | The birth of the Child of Promise, the God reborn, the beginning of the death of winter |
| Imbolc | Imbolc | 31st January – 1st February | The first signs of spring, and the Goddess returns to the earth |
| Alban Eilir | Ostara | The spring equinox, around 21st March | Spring is sprung! The Child of Promise is conceived |
| Beltane | Beltane | 30th April – 1st May | The sacred marriage of the God and Goddess |
| Alban Hefin | Litha | The summer solstice, around 21st June | The God reaches his highest power – and begins his decline |
| Lughnasadh | Lughnasadh | 1st August | Harvest, and the death of the God |
| Alban Elfed | Mabon | The autumn equinox, around 21st September | The second harvest and the approach to winter |
| Samhuinn | Samhain | 31st October | The festival of the dead |

# AICME 1

## Beith ┰ *Birth and New Beginnings.*

The first *few* of the first aicme, Beith corresponds to our letter B. Pronounced BEH or BETH.

**Tree:** The birch: *Betula pendula* and other *Betula spp.*

**Female**

**Rune:** Berkana.

**Tarot:** The Fool, the court cards of the suit of Swords.

**Qabalah:** Beth, the 12th path.

**Deity(ies):** Brigid of the Forge, Bride, Arianrhod, Frigga and Freyja, maiden and mother Goddesses generally, Thor.

**Correspondences:** Colours: white and silver. Crystal: white quartz.

**Planet:** Venus.

**Element:** Air.

**Sabbat:** Birch is associated with the interval between Yule and Imbolc, but also with Beltane (maypoles are commonly made from birch, which is a hermaphrodite tree).

**Living Things:** Snowdrops, celandines, daisies, fly agaric, plovers, stags, cows, white animals and white birds.

The **silver birch** has wound itself into the hearts of people across the world, especially gardeners, who value it for its astonishing beauty. Its gleaming white trunk, shapely glittering leaves and weeping habit make this small tree an icon of arboreal beauty, a real Lady of the Woods. She speaks of early spring, for that is her heyday, and is so clearly feminine, wearing her gracile twigs like jewellery.

**Range:** Betula species are found across the world from Siberia to Africa, from Eastern Europe to the Americas and Asia, so this tree is familiar to most people on Earth. Its grace and beauty have made it popular as a garden and park tree, particularly the variety known from its papery white bark as "silver birch" – *Betula pendula*. The tree does not achieve great height, yet despite its apparent fragility it can withstand some extremes of weather and is a *pioneer tree*, that is, one of the first trees to appear in previously damaged habitats. Although it has a relatively short life span (usually around 80 years) it has been with us a long time and was one of the first trees to appear after the last Ice Age. Important to many cultures, it is especially valued by the Russians, who have adopted it as their national tree.

Whilst the birch is found there as well, in China the bird plum or sweet plum *Sageretia theezans* (an ornamental evergreen shrub) shares the meaning of new beginnings, and as a Bonsai is often given as a gift when a baby is born.

**Healing Properties:** The birch is appropriately clad in white like a twentieth century nurse, for this beautiful tree has many healing properties, starting with its almost magical ability to heal wounds. The Native Americans were long aware of this and used birch bark dressings on injuries: the plant appears to speed up healing of damaged tissue and the formation of scar tissue. The sap, which is tapped and collected in early spring as it starts to flow, can also be used to sooth inflamed skin and rashes. The bark, laid on aching muscles, will ease the pain. Europeans have belatedly wised up to this and a medicinal gel made from birch bark has recently been approved for use on external injuries in the EU.

Birch sap has traditionally been made into wine or drunk as a tonic and is known to have a beneficial effect on the kidneys; and women who have suffered the excruciating misery of cystitis will be interested to hear that the sap and leaves are a remedy for urinary infections. This syrupy sap, which is said to taste very similar to maple syrup, is a folk remedy for rheumatism and gout. The tender, juicy inner bark can be eaten and is sometimes cut into strips and cooked like pasta. The betulinic acid found in the sap is used in the treatment of cancer (and also cancer in horses). The sap can be used as a shampoo!

**Uses:** Birch is musical! Its wood is used for musical instruments, such as guitars and drums, as well as in the making of speaker cabinets which require wood with a special resonance, also in mallets for keyboards.

The wood is nowadays used for the manufacture of paper, but before that the white bark was often used to write on, and birch bark manuscripts survive in museums across the world.

Birching was a historic punishment for adults and children alike; a bundle of birch (or other flexible twigs) was part of the equipment of Victorian schoolmasters, and the birching of offenders went on until the 1970s on the Isle of Man, the last British Crown dependency to allow this.

Today, birch twigs are still used percussively in a rather more pleasurable way; to stimulate people enjoying a traditional Scandinavian sauna.

**Myth and Story:** Not surprisingly, this beautiful tree is important in folklore and spiritual belief and in some cultures it is seen as a world tree, as the ash tree is in Norse belief – shamans would climb it in search of inspiration and for its connections to the worlds above and below. It appears as a manifestation of the sorcerer Gwydion, a colossal figure in Celtic belief, equivalent to Merlin in the Arthurian legends. In the cryptic mediaeval poem, *Cad Goddeu* (Battle of the Trees), the trees themselves mobilise to fight on Gwydion's side against Arawn, God of the Underworld, who is angry because a dog, a lapwing and a roebuck have been stolen from him. Gwydion himself is the birch tree, who leads the trees into battle and, being a magical being, has the power to restore them to life if they are killed. No one is entirely sure what the poem means, but *The White Goddess* author, Robert Graves, saw in it an enumeration of the trees represented in the Ogham.

In Celtic belief, the tree's white trunk marks it out as an entrance to the Otherworld and the world of the Fae – just as trees with white blossoms and red berries and white animals are seen as otherworldly. The fly agaric toadstool (*Amanita muscaria*), used in shamanic trancework, thrives under birch trees, adding another layer to the tree's mystical qualities. This fungus – the iconic red and white one associated with fairies and gnomes in pictures and animations – is also a traditional component of the infamous witches' flying ointment, while the birch itself was used in making the besom or broom.

In Wales, people traditionally made their babies' cradles from birch wood, as this would bring in the energies of the Goddess to protect the child.

**Magic:** Use birch for magical and spiritual protection in the sense of cleansing; have the *few* Beith or the tree's twigs and leaves on your altar or burn the dried bark and twigs as incense for cleansing. Use Beith as a magical sigil in all spells of cleansing and new beginnings, and use a birch besom to physically cleanse your home at certain times – at Imbolc or perhaps when there has been negativity in the home for some reason, such as a quarrel or some ill-fortune; or to sweep away the remnants of the old year and welcome in a new one. Use the birch also to sweep away fears and create courage. Decorate the tree itself, or a branch of it, to celebrate the spring Sabbats of Imbolc, Ostara and Beltane.

A birch wand can be used to invoke Bride, Freyja (or other maiden or mother Goddesses) and also Gods to whom it is sacred, such as Thor and Lugh.

Birch essential oil is a useful ingredient of love spells and can also be used to anoint your tools to cleanse and empower them.

**Divination:** The meaning of this *few* is new beginnings, regeneration and even actual birth. While this *few* is the first letter of the Ogham alphabet and yew (death and endings) is the last, it is better to consider the series as a circle, rather than a line. So, this *few* may also indicate rebirth and regeneration, or new beginnings of other kinds; new journeys, a new career, a new relationship, a new home. Remembering its career path as a broom, it is easy to see how this tree can mean new starts, purification, clearing out the old to make way for the new, the clearing of blockages and also initiation. *Put the past behind you,* says this Ogham; *clear away dead wood, lose what you no longer need, and look to the future – don't be afraid of the new things and experiences that are coming.*

**Reversed:** The *few* speaks of the danger of stagnation and holding onto the past, to things, feelings and ideas you no longer need.

## *Visualisation Story*

You are walking along a narrow path through snow-filled woods. Admire the beauty of the virgin snow covering every inch of the woodland floor and lodged in the branches of the trees. A low wintry sun casts a reddish glow on the snow, throwing the shadows of trees long distances behind them: it is the shortest day of the year. As you walk, the trees thin out a little and eventually the path leads you to the edge of the wood and a snow-clad field beyond. A solitary tree stands there, a silver birch, its trunk as white as the snow beneath.

The Sun has risen a little higher. You observe a tree stump near the birch and walk over to it, sitting on it to rest. The tree is before you, its slender twigs seeming to glitter in the wintry light. The air seems to have grown a little warmer, and the Sun has risen a little higher in the sky.

You are sitting meditatively, lost in your own thoughts, when you observe a small tremor in the snow just below the base of the birch tree. As you watch, a small piece of the snow lifts and falls aside, revealing a bright green bud. The bud grows upwards, sprouts some long green leaves, then it opens, revealing a snowdrop, whiter than the snow. The flower continues to grow and swell and then it lifts its head and opens. Inside the flower lies a tiny newborn child, perfectly formed and healthy. As you look on the child, memories stir within you ... family photographs come to your mind, and you realise this child is you – reborn and full of promise, and that its message to you is that there are always opportunities for new starts.

Alternatively, according to your own beliefs, you can see the baby as the newborn Child of Promise, the Star Child, who is the God, reborn to the Goddess after dying at harvest time and heralding in a new year – a new journey.

## *Luis* ╥ *Protection.*

Corresponds to our letter L.

Pronounced LWEESH or LOOSH.

**Tree:** The rowan: *Sorbus spp.*, particularly the European rowan: *Sorbus aucuparia.*

**Female**

**Rune:** Algiz.

**Tarot:** The High Priestess.

**Qabalah:** Daleth, the 4th path.

**Deity(ies):** Bride, Cernunnos, Herne, Lugh, Nementona, Heimdallr, Thor and his wife Sif.

**Correspondences:** Colours: red and green. Crystals: ruby and tourmaline.

**Planets:** The Sun and Mercury.

**Element:** Fire.

**Sabbat:** Imbolc.

**Living Things:** Snowdrops, bears, unicorns, ducks and quail.

All trees are beautiful but the **rowan** lays some claim to being the most attractive and graceful of all, with its slender shape, its delicate lace-edged leaves and its pretty blossom and fruit. A fairy tree, it is mentioned in so many stories of fairies and magic that to look on the tree is to see all kinds of things in your imagination. It is a fairy queen, crowned with blossom and decked out in lace.

**Range:** Also known as the "quicken tree", its ability to grow at high altitudes and cling to rocky crags gives it the name "mountain ash" and it has also been called "Lady of the Mountains." This tree loves cool high locations and is found across Northern Europe, the Himalayas and Tibet and into China. It is quite happy on lower ground though and it has become a very popular addition to gardens – its small size makes it ideal even for modest-sized gardens – and parks. Like the birch, it is a pioneer tree, growing before other species on previously damaged or disturbed soil.

In regions where rowan is not found, other trees believed to protect against evil and harm include palms, peach trees, gingkoes and cypresses.

**Healing Properties:** With antioxidants galore and large amounts of vitamin C and beta carotene, the berries are a superfood, though they should not be eaten raw. They have been shown to have a beneficial effect on diabetes and are anti-inflammatory, and this, plus the large amount of fibre they contain, makes them helpful for IBS sufferers. The berries are also excellent for sore throats, coughs and colds and they can stop a cold in its tracks. The berries are antibacterial and a tea made from them or the flowers will soothe the digestion and act as a laxative. One study showed that taking rowan berries with bamboo in a tea alleviated hair loss.

**Uses:** *Sorbus domestica* was once common in the UK, grown for its edible fruit, but mankind has become less adventurous with the onset of supermarkets and their insistence on selling us strawberries in winter – this tree is now almost unknown here. Wild rowan berries are edible but vilely sour and bitter and they do contain toxins which can lead to upset stomachs when the berries are eaten raw. They can actually cause quite serious illness if taken in any quantity, so they are best cooked for consumption. As well as fruit pies and puddings, the fruit is used for making jams, jellies and pickles to accompany meats and cheeses, wines, fruit liqueurs and cordials, and is also used as a flavouring in ales.

The slender but hard wood is easily carved and is used for handles and walking sticks, and even for larger agricultural items, such as rakes. The bark and berries are used in dyeing and the ancient Druids once used them for dyeing their ceremonial robes.

**Myth and Story:** This elegant little tree has long been seen as magical by the Celtic nations, who regarded trees and shrubs that bear white blossom and red berries as being connected with the Otherworld and the Fae, as red and white are the colours of the Fairy Kingdom. The regard the Druids had for it (and modern Druids still have) is evidenced by another of its names – Druid's Tree. In Scotland, the use of any part of this sacred tree (with the exception of the fruit) was once forbidden for anything but magical or ritual purposes and it goes without saying that cutting down a rowan or even damaging it was seen as likely to bring much ill-fortune to the perpetrator. It shares with elder the supposed distinction of having been used to make Christ's Cross (highly unlikely in either case, due to their small size and scanty timber, plus the fact that they are not native to Jerusalem). The tree was said to ward off witches (we aren't sure about that one, as the berries have a tiny pentacle on the blossom end – the symbol of paganism!) and keep the Devil at bay, and sprigs of rowan were fastened over cowsheds and stables to protect the animals. They were also carried by people as a protection against witches and magic.

In Norse mythology, the first woman, Embla, was either created from a rowan or an elm (the first man, Askr, being created from an ash) and the rowan was sacred to Thor, as it was said to have spread its branches down to rescue him from a river which was sweeping him away.

In Classical mythology, the rowan sprang from the white feathers and blood drops of an eagle sent to retrieve Hebe's magical cup from demons who had stolen it, who clearly put up a fight before the bird was able to return the vessel to its owner.

A very simple example of foretelling using the rowan is the old country saying that a heavy crop of fruit means a bad winter; however, the rowan shares this supposed property with many other wild fruit trees and shrubs and this has little basis in fact. The fruits grow well in a good summer, which does not always presage a bad winter.

**Magic:** This tree speaks of divination, magic, insight and inspiration and was seen as a doorway by the Celts, either to the Otherworld or to knowledge and inspiration. Ogham *fews* were commonly made from its twigs, and it is a good choice if you are unable to collect twigs from all the appropriate trees. Its principal use is for protection and this can be utilised by growing the tree near the home, especially at the front door or the front gate to the property, or by carrying its components about the person or placing them in the home, especially at the doors and windows. Take a rowan staff with you when you go walking, for protection and for aid against getting lost, for this is another virtue of this tree: it protects and guides the traveller. A very simple example of a protection spell is to take two short rowan twigs and bind them into an equal-armed, or solar, cross with red ribbon or wool and then hang it in the porch or under the eaves. For modern pagans, it is easy to hide this item in a hanging basket so that visitors are completely unaware of its presence, or to make a very small version which can be carried in a pocket for protection outside the home. Because of its innate healing properties, the tree can also be used for magical healing; for example, the practice of hanging up a few berries tied in a cloth against any illness "doing the rounds."

**Divination:** Its most important meaning is protection – of the powerful protection the tree can offer, and of safety and even home. It is the *few* of guidance and of not getting lost as the tree, perhaps because of its singular beauty, was seen as a guide to travellers – the wayfarer's tree. This letter urges you to trust in your own intuition and inspiration, to find your own way with its magical protection. You are "home safe".

**Reversed:** The *few* can speak of being lost and without guidance or protection, that you are not safe and need to take steps to protect yourself.

## Visualisation Story

You find yourself alone in a dark forest at dusk, silent apart from the cries of owls and the wind moaning through the branches. You are terribly afraid, starting at each new sound from the darkness. You walk on through the forest, which becomes darker and more threatening, and it seems as though roots deliberately catch at your feet, trying to trip you. The screeching of the owls grows louder and more eldritch and you become aware that you are hopelessly lost.

In the undergrowth behind you there is now movement, the sound of a large creature moving in the bushes, and you are sure you heard a low growl. Your fear increases and you hurry on, faster now, your breath catching in your throat from fear. As you go, you take a moment to call on the Goddess for help.

Ahead of you now you think you perceive a patch of light, perhaps the Moon shining down through the branches into a small clearing, and you hasten towards it, hearing the sounds of the large animal behind you growing closer and more purposeful. The light grows stronger as you approach, and you keep to the track, which appears to grow smoother and broader as you approach the light. The light grows and the sounds of the animal behind you grow fainter as you approach and find the light shining into a small clearing, where a dainty rowan tree stands in the centre, holding up its branches to the Moon.

Breathing hard now, and even more aware of the danger you have just been in, you stagger towards the tree and place a hand on its lowest branch, looking up into its graceful branches with gratitude and hope. To your surprise, the branch comes away in your hand and you find yourself holding a slender but sturdy staff, which gives off a faint light of its own.

You thank the tree from the bottom of your heart and set off on the forest track again, knowing the magical staff will not only protect you from animals lurking nearby but will light your way and lead you towards home and safety.

## *Fearn* ᚈ *Counsel, Guidance and Support.*

Corresponds to our letter F or V.
Pronounced FAIR-n.
**Tree:** The alder: *Alnus glutinosa*.
**Male**
**Rune:** Ansuz and Mannaz.
**Tarot:** All four suits.
**Deity(ies):** Aries, Arthur, Cronos, Odin, Mars, Mercury/Hermes, Thoth.
**Correspondences:** Colours: green, purple and red. Crystals: amethyst and lapis lazuli. **Planet:** Venus.
**Element:** Earth, air, fire and water.
**Sabbat:** Alban Eilir/Ostara.
**Living Things:** The raven and crow, seagulls, fox, hawk, broom.

The tall and stately **alder** is not as recognisable as some of our native trees, and its leaves closely resemble – and can be confused with – those of hazel, to which it is closely related. Look for it in marshy places and feel its contentment at being there; if it is stranded in a dry place it may give off quite piteous vibes.

**Range:** This thirsty, water-loving tree inhabits most of Europe, including the UK, only excepting the extreme north and south, and thrives in wetlands, bogs and the banks of rivers, streams and lakes. Although it will grow in drier conditions and in quite poor soil, it is not happy far from water and will not produce seeds: it is the only British deciduous tree to produce cones. While only the common or black alder, *Alnus glutinosa*, is found in the UK, other alder species grow in locations across the world where the climate is cooler, including in the Americas, Russia, Asia (including mountainous regions like Tibet) and the Mediterranean, and has migrated in the last century down as far as South Africa. Introduced into Australia for ornamental purposes, the black alder has been so successful as to be considered a significant environmental pest. It is a large and impressive tree, and although it is not especially long-lived, it can achieve up to 30 metres in height. The UK species of alder, *Alnus glutinosa*, is also regarded as a pioneer tree.

**Healing Properties:** Like the willow, alder bark contains salicin – the basis of aspirin. Like birch, to which it is also related, some species of alder contain betulin, which has been used in the treatment of tumours. A tea made from the bark and leaves can treat headaches, fevers, sore throats and skin rashes, and also acts as an anti-inflammatory on wounds, rashes and haemorrhoids. The leaves are soothing when laid on burns and nettle stings (and more efficacious still if they are ground to a paste before being applied), and travellers have used the leaves inside their shoes to soothe tired feet and protect against blisters.

**Uses:** The flowers of alder have been used to produce a green dye. The wood is very long-lasting in water, and it was used to create the foundations of Venice, where it has lasted many centuries! Because of its oily, water-resistant nature, it has also been used to build bridges and fashion buckets and other containers for liquids, and also for furniture veneers. The bark is also rich in tannin, and is used in the leather industry, while the hard timber is used in the production of furniture and clogs. The countryfolk of old would lay down the leaves, which are rather sticky, in henhouses and animal sheds to attract and catch fleas and other pests.

**Myth and Story:** Alder is the symbol of Bran the Blessed in Celtic legends, the magical Welsh king who features in many stories and whose head is said to have been buried beneath the Tower of London to keep Britain's enemies away; it is clear he inspired some of the Arthurian legends as well.

When cut, the alder's pale wood turns a deep orange, which gives the impression it is bleeding. This caused the tree to be seen as magical and also unlucky by the Celts, and the Irish once believed it was unlucky even to pass an alder tree on their travels. In common with other trees, alder was seen as special to the Fae, who inhabited the tree or used it as a gateway on their way to the Otherworld, and there are folk tales of people being taken by the Fae and a log of alder wood left in their place. It was believed that a flute made from alder wood could summon fairies. The alder was also believed to be the home of the spirits of men who had drowned – another reason for treating it with respect.

**Magic:** Alder is a protective tree and amulets made from its twigs can be carried for protection, especially in a situation in which you do not feel confident. Use the tree or the *few* in magic to mend friendships and bring peace and amity, also to increase courage and self-confidence and decrease anxiety. An incense made from the twigs will disperse negative energies.

**Divination:** The magic and meaning of this tree lies in its association with being a bridge – between worlds, between elements, between people. The living tree bridges earth and water, water and sky, sky and earth, and all these and fire, as it is ruled by all four elements. It is easy to imagine a dying alder falling across a stream or river, as they must often do, and becoming a bridge indeed for travellers wishing to cross. But the story of Bran gives another meaning to this *few*: according to legend, his head continued to talk as it was being carried to its final resting place in London, giving advice and counsel to those who journeyed with it, and this tells us Fearn is associated with knowledge, advice and with bridging of another kind – between people. It is the *few* of communication, of interaction, of benefiting from the wisdom of others and allowing them to benefit from your own, of mending or maintaining bridges between yourself and others, or between people who have quarrelled or are in dispute. Alder or Fearn is spoken of as a shield in the Cad Goddeu, and so this *few* speaks of protection in the sense of friends coming to your defence, of being supported. The idea of Bran's head, buried under the Tower of London to keep away Britain's foes, reinforces this idea of protection.

Fearn also calls on you to trust your own judgement and to have faith in yourself, to be the hero you always knew you were. But it also tells you that an advisor is at hand and you should be open to counsel, perhaps from an older, wiser person; or that you may be called upon yourself to advise others.

**Reversed:** The *few* speaks of blockages to advice, perhaps a warning to you to open your ears and stop being pig-headed!

## *Visualisation Story*

Some matter is troubling you, and you are muttering to yourself and worrying about it as you travel through pleasant fields, wondering where in the world you might find someone to advise you on the best course. The pathway between the meadows is light and sandy and easy for your feet, and you hardly notice when it begins to slope downwards.

The terrain becomes a little less easy; the path is muddy now and there are large pools of muddy water to either side, which soon begin to impinge on the track itself, so that occasionally you have to skip or leap to avoid getting your shoes wet. But your mind is so full of your troubles that you barely notice this, except as one more nuisance to vex you.

Suddenly you come to a fork in the path, where it divides into three or four little paths that wander off in different directions. Because the meadows here are full of slopes and small clumps of trees, it is not possible to see which path takes you to where you want to go. You mutter a curse, furious at the difficulty.

Along the path behind you comes an older person, walking with the aid of a stout pale wooden staff – it is alder wood. You turn and look closely at this traveller, an older man with a long white beard and twinkling eyes. He wears a bunch of sticky alder leaves in his hatband to protect him from flies and other insects. They glisten and catch the light. You feel your anger and frustration subside as you realise this is a wise person to whom you can turn for advice. A friend in need; you instinctively feel he knows these lands as well as anyone and maybe walks them every day. He stops and you stand and look at one another.

"Excuse me, sir, but which path will take me to the town?" you ask him politely. He smiles so widely that his twinkling eyes almost disappear in his wrinkled cheeks and he points to the path directly ahead. For a moment you are tempted to argue: you know the town lies to the east, away from the river, but this path seems to lead straight to the water.

At once you decide to trust him and take the path he has shown you, and with this decision comes a new thought. The old man walks beside you now, saying nothing, but exuding an air of friendliness. After a while, you take a decision and begin to talk to him, mentioning the thing which has been on your mind. The old man says nothing for a long time and, as you walk the path you are on, it leads to the river and over a wooden bridge before it turns sharply and heads in another direction. When he does speak, it is a simple remark about trusting your own instincts. Before long, you see the roofs of the town rising before you and the matter that was troubling you has resolved itself in your mind.

## Saille ‖‖‖ Dreams, Intuition, Magic.

Corresponds to our letter S.
Pronounced SHAIL-uh or SHARL-yuh.
**Tree:** The willow: *Salix spp.*
**Female**
**Rune:** Laguz.
**Tarot:** The Moon, Queen of Cups.
**Qabalah:** Qoph, the 29th path.
**Deity(ies):** Artemis, Bride, the Cailleach, Cerridwen, Diana, Hecate, the Morrigan, Selene and all Goddesses of the Moon and magic.
**Correspondences:** Colour: grey. Crystals: moonstone/selenite.
**Planet:** The Moon.
**Element:** Water.
**Sabbat:** Imbolc.
**Living Things:** Hawks, deer, owls, rabbits and hares, primroses.

The **willow** is a most elegant and feminine tree with its slender branches and long trailing leaves, all in subtle shades of pale green and grey. Lining a riverbank or drooping beautifully in a garden, it has a very magical and spiritual look and has always been associated with Goddesses.

**Range:** The 400-odd species of willow, which range from small shrubs to large trees, are found in countries throughout the world, from the Northern Hemisphere to North Africa and the Middle and Far East, and are classified as pioneer trees – some were planted in Australia in the twentieth century and have thrived so completely that they are now considered an invasive pest. Even South America has its own species: the Chilean willow, *Salix humboldtiana*, which grows throughout the continent and North America. All willows love to live by water.

**Healing Properties:** One of our most common remedies, aspirin, derives originally from the bark of the willow, which is rich in salicin and was once infused in hot water to provide relief from headaches, pain and fevers. The tree heals pain on non-physical levels as well and is a Bach remedy for those who have suffered sorrow. The bark of the tree is antibacterial and can be used to sterilise dressings.

**Uses:** The best-known use for willow is wicker basket weaving, which is still a thriving industry today, but a popular – if somewhat ephemeral – by-product of this craft is the willow sculpture, examples of which exist all over the UK. In the past, before plastic carriers, willow baskets were used for everything; now they are valued as a charming and decorative container for everything from cutlery to laundry to potted plants. Cricket bats are made from willow, also furniture, whistles, some veneers, walking sticks, handles and brooms. In recent times, as "green burials" have become popular, coffins have been made from wicker – revisiting its association with death and mourning. Black willow, or pussy willow, has become a much-loved component of floral bouquets.

**Myth and Story:** The willow's most important correspondence is its connection to the Moon, which makes a wand made from its wood a must for any witch.

Famously, those in mourning, particularly for a lost lover, wore a piece of willow in their hatband. The "weeping willow" may take its name from this or from its pendulous habit, commonly over water, where it is mirrored in the surface. The Victorians were fond of depicting this beautiful tree on gravestones and mourning jewellery, seeing it as the embodiment of grief and mourning. The ever-popular Willow Pattern china shows a willow and an apple tree as part of its decorations, the design supposedly telling the story of two lovers fleeing from a vengeful magician.

**Magic:** Willow is the wand of choice for many witches because of its association with Hecate, Mother of Witches, and with the Moon. Willow was also traditionally used to bind the birchen twigs onto a broom, because of their flexibility, and it is thus an integral part of the magical besom. It is used for protective banishing magic and for work to alleviate grief and sadness, also for love spells. It can also be used, like the hazel, for water divining.

**Divination:** Willow speaks of human emotions and psychic intuition, of dreams, of feminine wisdom and tradition, of witches and magic. Sacred to Hecate, it is very special to witches, who often own a willow wand in preference to any other wood. Turning up this *few* may mean you are making progress on your spiritual path, or that you should do so. It is a reassuring Ogham, though it can mean a sudden outpouring of emotion, perhaps a catharsis. It can also mean a sudden inspiration, perhaps in work or in art. Whatever the question you have asked, this Ogham suggests you are influenced by intuition and that insights gained this way can be trusted, and you should open yourself to your more spiritual, intuitive side. Perhaps magic is the answer to your problem, but if it is, tread carefully and use your spiritual perceptions rather than rushing in gung-ho, as your own instincts will tell you how to proceed. If your question has been about others, this *few* may identify a (usually) female person, perhaps an older, wise woman who has been or could be an influence on you.

**Reversed:** This *few* may speak of enchantments affecting you, or warn you against over-emotionalism and fanciful ideas, that daydreams are not a substitute for real life.

## *Visualisation Story*

It is late at night, and you are strolling along the bank of a river, watching the moonlight gleam on the surface, breaking into glints and gleams here and there, where the water flows over or around an obstruction. The Moon herself is hanging in the branches of an ancient willow that leans down precariously over the stream as though it is debating with itself whether to slide in. As you draw near to the tree, you see a pale form beside it and a woman in a long white or silver dress is revealed, leaning low over the water with one hand on the willow's trunk, while the other trails in the water.

As you approach, she straightens up and stands awaiting you, still with one hand upon the tree. She has long fair or white hair that hangs over her shoulders and down her back, and a pale, oval face with large, bright eyes. You are not sure if she is a young girl or a very old woman, although her slim body and upright stance incline you to think the former. She leaves the tree and comes towards you; you notice with a strange lack of surprise that she does not walk but floats an inch or so above the ground, her long silvery dress flowing behind her. Enraptured by her beauty, you watch her approach, her large dark eyes fixed on your face. As she comes closer, you can still not decide whether she is a beautiful young girl or a dazzling older woman; she seems to change from one to the other as you watch, without changing her appearance in the least.

Reaching you, she wordlessly hands you a small wooden box with a carved spiral symbol on the lid – a gift for you. Opening it, you find a complete set of the Ogham *fews* inside, each beautifully finished; they seem to glow under the Moon's light. You raise your eyes to her face and she nods and smiles. You understand what she is telling you; that this is a sign for you to continue your magical work with her blessing. You bow before her and thank her.

## Nion ꜰꜰꜰꜰ Courage and Self-mastery.

Corresponds to our letter N.
Pronounced NEE-un.
**Tree:** The ash: *Fraxinus excelsior*.
**Male**
**Rune:** Teiwaz.
**Tarot:** The Hanged Man
**Qabalah:** Peh, the 17th path.
**Deity(ies):** Eostra, Frigga, Hel, Holle, Lir/Manannan, Minerva/Athena, Nemesis, Neptune/Poseidon, Odin.
**Correspondences**: Colours: pale blue, white and green. Crystal: turquoise. The sea.
**Planet:** The Sun.
**Element:** Fire and water.
**Sabbat:** Alban Eilir/Ostara.
**Living Things:** Sea creatures, particularly seahorses, snakes, snipe and wood anemones.

The **ash** is a large and stately tree that will be familiar to most people. Its appearance is very clean limbed: its grey bark smooth as human skin and its branches and trunk straight as a ruler. It stands proud.

**Range:** The European ash, a large forest tree if left without coppicing, is found across the temperate zone and is the tree found in British hedgerows and woods, but up to 65 species of ash are known across Europe, North America and Asia. Sadly, it has fallen victim in recent years to two plagues: the emerald ash-borer beetle and the ash dieback fungus. In 2016, the ash was described as in danger of extinction due to the latter.

The ash is related to the olive tree, which is known across a wide range of countries in the Mediterranean, Asia and Africa and is now commercially grown in countries in which it did not occur naturally, such as the Americas. Olive trees are extremely important to the economy of the Mediterranean region and to individual families, who may see the often very aged trees as members of their families. Diane says a male and female tree may often grow or be grafted together, and this is known as a "grandmother and grandfather olive tree." Where the ash as Nion is about courage without violence, the olive is deeply associated with peace: we speak of "holding out an olive branch" as a first move to heal a quarrel.

**Healing Properties:** The ash has long been used for folk healing, from passing a sick child through a hole in the tree to charming warts from a person's face into the bark. Tisanes made from the leaves have been used as a laxative and also for a remedy for jaundice, bladder problems, gout and rheumatism.

**Uses:** Ash wood is well known for burning when green, and is prized as firewood, ash faggots having been used for stoves and open fires for centuries. Walter de la Mare famously wrote of it:

> *"Of all the trees in England,*
> *Her three sweet corners in,*
> *Only the ash, the bonny ash,*
> *Burns fierce while it is green."*

The wood is tough and durable, and has been used for many things, notably as fuel, the trees being coppiced to provide faggots and also long poles for brooms, agricultural tools, musical instruments and sports equipment, such as bows and tennis rackets. In the past, it was the prime choice for making a spear or arrows. The green wood, which is very resistant to splitting, was used as the base for rush-seated chairs. It is still used to make the wooden chassis of the famous UK-manufactured Morgan car.

**Myth and Story:** Probably the most famous example of an ash tree in mythology is the cosmic tree Yggdrasil in Norse belief, the vast tree which carries on its branches and among its roots all the nine worlds of men, Gods and other supernatural beings. Odin hanged himself on this tree over the Well of Wyrd, to gain the knowledge of the runes. An ash tree was also seen as the origin of the first man, Askr, who was created from one of these trees.

The ash was seen as protective by the Norsemen and the Celts and is commonly found planted by holy wells in the UK. One of the meanings of its name is "wave" – which may explain its association with the sea and with sea travel, or the connection could be that it was sacred to Poseidon. It was associated with the magician Gwydion, an important figure in Celtic belief, who was said to carry an ash staff as his symbol.

In Christian tradition, children would carry the ash twigs on Ash Wednesday, as they might carry acorns on Oak Apple Day, although the festival's name refers to the ashes of a fire, which were smeared on churchgoers' foreheads as part of the ritual.

**Magic:** Ash leaves scattered in the corners will protect a house, and an ash wand can be used in protective magic. The tree lends you its strength and courage, to protect yourself and those you love, and to stand up for what you believe.

Ash was and is prized for magical staffs by the Druids and a 2,000-year-old ash staff bound with copper was discovered on Anglesey, or Ynys Mon (where the Roman massacre of the Druids took place in 61CE), and is now in use by the Welsh Gorsedh, of which HRH Prince Charles is a supporter.

**Divination:** Nion is a spear; take it into your hand and go forward upon your path, filled with strength and self-mastery. This *few* tells you to know your own strength and the advantages you have been given, whether this is your own knowledge or the protection and help given by good friends. Take courage and walk towards what you know is right, turning away from that which would harm you or others. This Ogham is connected to the web of fate and knows you can influence your own fate and that of others, so take care that your actions are righteous and your intentions good, for fate and karma – *wyrd* and *orlog* – hang in the balance. Become more yourself and less a patsy or a victim to others. This *few* speaks of courage in travel, of going forth boldly and journeying across the sea as well as over land, never faltering in your purpose or doubting yourself, following the destiny that is yours.

**Reversed:** Take charge of your life, says this stave – you may have to delay plans until you are more in control of matters.

## Visualisation Story

A child is walking along a village path. He is a cute little boy with curly hair and a chubby face, but his shoulders are bent and he does not look happy. He is walking with his elder brother, who is perhaps three or four years older, and who has the hint of mischief in his eyes.

As the children go along, they see a garden over the hedge with ripe red apples and tempting yellow pears on the branches of the trees inside. There is no one in sight, the gate stands open and the elder boy goes inside, beckoning his brother. The young one does not want to do this; he stays outside the gate, looking very miserable, knowing he will get into trouble as he has a dozen times before, and that his brother will give him all the blame; perhaps saying, as he has before, that he himself only went into the garden to fetch his brother out from where he should not have been.

"Come on!" says the older boy, "Don't you want some of this fruit? It's just hanging on the trees, going to waste; no one is picking it."

"It's not our garden and not our fruit. We'll get in trouble," replies the smaller boy.

"Don't be such a scaredy-cat," sneers his brother, and proceeds to tease and insult him until the younger boy has tears in his eyes and has actually started walking towards the open gate, so upset and ashamed is he by his brother's contempt for his honest principles.

As he walks, his eyes sadly on the ground, a falling leaf blows onto his shoe. He stops and picks it up: it is a little yellow ash leaf, like a row of little oval coins on a thin stem. He raises it to his eyes and stares at it, ignoring his brother's impatient urgings from inside the garden.

It is as though the leaf is a message from the tree, a stately ash that stands a few yards away from the garden gate. He straightens up and looks around at the tree, noticing it properly, perhaps for the first time. He sees how straight the trunk is, how straight the branches, even how straight the small twigs are. It is as though the tree stands up defiantly, raising its head, refusing to be bowed or dictated to by anyone, and this feeling comes over the boy in a rush of realisation.

He turns to the gate and shouts to his brother, "You can get into trouble if you want, I'm going home."

"Going to tell on me?" sneers the brother.

"No, I won't tell, but from now on if you want to do bad things, you do them by yourself. I'm not like you and I won't be made to do them. Goodbye."

He goes, his head and shoulders raised and looking much happier than he did before. His brother watches him go, his mouth slightly open, clearly realising that this is a turning point in their relationship.

# AICME 2

## *Uath (sometimes Huath)* ⊥ *Difficulty, Humiliation, Pain, also Romance.*

First *few* of the second aicme, Uath corresponds to our letter H.

Pronounced OO-wah.

**Tree:** The hawthorn, whitethorn or maytree, *Crataegus monogyna.*

**Male**

**Rune:** Thurisaz.

**Tarot:** The World.

**Qabalah:** Kaph, the 21st path.

**Deity(ies):** Cardea/Flora, Belenus, Blodeuwedd, Flora, the Green Man, Hera and Juno, Hymen, Maia, Persephone.

**Correspondences:** Colours: midnight blue and purple. Crystals: lapis lazuli and blue calcite.

**Planets:** Mars and Venus.

**Element:** Fire.

**Sabbat:** Beltane.

**Living Things:** Blackbirds, owls, martins and wood sorrel.

The **hawthorn** is surely the most familiar of all our hedgerow trees and filled with childhood memories. It is a little tree, not getting very tall, even when not subject to autumn hedge-cutting, but its bright red berries and many of its red autumn leaves linger long into the winter. A friend to wildlife of all kinds, it is a long-lived tree and older specimens can look very eldritch with their twisted, lichen-encrusted branches.

**Range:** Hawthorn species are found across the world, over most of Europe, Asia (where several evergreen species are found), North Africa and the US. The thorn is hardy and survives in regions of high winds (where other trees would be felled by the blast before they achieved any height) by stunting itself and leaning away from the wind, bending where other trees would break – a lesson for us all? Its flexible timber also helps preserve it. It will grow in any soils, even very poor ones.

The tree could be aligned with any thorny tree with healing properties in countries where it does not naturally occur.

**Healing Properties:** The country children who supplemented their diet by nibbling on "bread-and-cheese", the tender new shoots of the hawthorn in spring, were wiser than they knew. This common hedgerow tree has amazing tonic and health-giving properties, including the ability to lower blood pressure, improve circulation and strengthen the heart's rhythm. Both the leaves and the berries, called "haws", are used for this in the form of a tea and it is possible to make or buy tincture of hawthorn, which can be taken as a few drops in a glass of water. It is a safe and gentle remedy. The fruit is also rich in vitamins C and B-complex.

**Uses:** The principal use of hawthorn in the countryside is for hedging, as its vicious thorns will keep out intruders and keep in livestock and it establishes in any soil and grows fast; hence one of its epithets: quickthorn. The hard, close-grained wood is good for turning, and was used for handles and other small items, as well as veneers. The bright red haws can be made into jellies but are very tasteless and stodgy and best left for the birds.

**Myth and Story:** Many folk beliefs surround the hawthorn, which is first and foremost a fairy tree, as its white blossom and red berries signify – although there is also a pink-blossomed variant, red may. Its association with Beltane, 1st May, goes back to before the current calendar was adjusted in 1752, when the tree did indeed bloom on this date and both greenery and blossom were used to deck the maypole and the May Queen, but it now blossoms in April.

Perhaps more than any other tree, it is used for the hanging of "clooties" and other gifts to appease the Fae and petition the

Gods. Unlucky to bring into the house – except on May Day – says one of the most well-known beliefs, possibly deriving from the old custom of laying May blossom on a coffin, where its strong, fishy, foetid but not entirely unpleasant aroma would cover any odour from the corpse. It is also considered very unlucky to cut down a thorn, because of its association with the fairies. In Christian mythology, Christ's Crown of Thorns was said to have been made from hawthorn.

One of the most famous examples of this tree is the Glastonbury Thorn, a twice-flowering variant that blooms at Christmas as well as in the spring, and is said to have grown there after Joseph of Arimathea planted his staff in British soil when he visited, possibly with the Christ child. However, the earliest mention in text of this tree is in the sixteenth century, so it is more likely that a crusader returning from the Holy Land brought it with him, either deliberately or as a staff which "took" when it was left in the ground on Wearyall Hill. Generations of scions have been struck from the original tree, which was cut down by Cromwell's supporters as a relic of superstition, and there are now several specimens in the Abbey grounds and local churchyards, whilst the descendant on Wearyall Hill has been struggling since it was vandalised in 2010. Abbey staff send a flowering branch to the Queen at Christmas.

**Magic:** Like almost all trees, hawthorn is protective – you have only to look at those vicious thorns to see where that idea came from! It is very useful in a protective talisman or a witch-bottle (these traditionally contained old nails, pins, needles and other sharp metal objects, but thorns are just as good). A tisane of the leaves can be used to sprinkle the home or sacred area to cleanse and protect, and a hawthorn wand has uses against evil spirits. The tree brings happiness and contentment, so is useful in work for someone who is perhaps depressed or has had a run of bad luck and is feeling "down".

**Divination:** The name of this thorny *few* translates as "horror" or "fright" and the tree is certainly a source of harm for anyone who comes up against it unaware. The Ogham *few* speaks of a mishap, of an encounter with harm and pain, and of the pain and damage that can befall those who rush in where angels fear to tread. This can be actual physical harm, such as the tree might inflict on you if you come up against it, or it could be mental distress, embarrassment, shame, humiliation and social disgrace that you might incur if you act without judgement and care. It speaks of difficult situations, but also of how these will pass if you do not act foolishly or aggressively.

Hawthorn and Uath are also deeply connected to human relationships, just as Beltane is a traditional time for handfastings and the "greenwood marriages" and *hieros gamos* of folklore. The blossoms are said to smell of sex and the plant contains a tonic for the heart, so may Uath speak of love, of attraction, romance, betrothal and marriage. Strange? But love and sex can be scary in their own way!

Just as there can be barriers to love, so in other areas of life the *few* speaks of problems on the way and urges caution and care, as you would need to approach this thorny customer!

**Reversed:** The *few* can tell of an obstacle in your path, which will need work and patience to get around, and of humiliation if you persist in using force and aggression to get your way.

## Visualisation Story

Justin is at his office's Christmas party. He didn't especially want to go, but he is a relatively new member of staff and he knows he should play ball. The office is hung with a few tatty streamers of tinsel and a plastic Christmas tree stands on a filing cabinet in the corner by the water cooler. Justin knows more or less everyone there and some of them have brought their partners; Justin broke up with his girlfriend a few weeks ago, so does not have anyone to bring. He knows he is going to be bored and uncomfortable at this event, but he promises himself he will stay for a while, just show his face and then plead an early start in the morning, as he plans on leaving early to go and visit his family in the Midlands for the Christmas holidays.

People are wandering about with plastic cups of punch in their hands, chatting and eating the dry-looking sausage rolls laid out on paper plates. The music is awful, what Justin calls "old people's home music" – some of it with a Christmas theme. Slade, for God's sake! And to cap it all, he has forgotten to bring his Secret Santa contribution, which will no doubt earn him a black mark from his boss.

Then he sees her. She is standing by the Christmas tree, on her own, quite clearly trying not to look bored. Tall, elegant, with dark floppy hair that falls into her eyes in such a sexy way. He has never seen her before, and he is instantly attracted to her. Taking his courage in his hands, he wanders over to her.

"Hello, I'm Justin from finance," he says.

She looks up slowly and smiles. "Simone," she says.

"Awful, awful party," he says, grinning. He has been told his grin is very sexy.

"Ye-es," she agrees slowly, "but you have to do your bit, don't you?"

"Or," he says, leaning closer to her and laying a hand on her arm, "We could just sneak out of here and go to the pub on the corner, and then perhaps on to a club?"

He isn't usually as aggressive as this with women, and he knows he has made a mistake as soon as the words are out of his mouth. Her face changes completely and then, to his unspeakable horror, he hears his boss's voice behind him.

"Are you all right, darling? Is this chap bothering you?"

## Duir ⏚ *Success, Achievement, Power, Renewal.*

Corresponds to our letter D.

Pronounced DOO-r.

**Tree:** The oak: *Quercus spp.*

**Male**

**Rune:** Raido.

**Tarot:** The Emperor.

**Qabalah:** Heh, the 15th path.

**Deity(ies):** Blodeuwedd, The Dagda, Jupiter, Taranis, Thor, Zeus.

**Correspondences:** Colours: gold and black. Crystals: diamond and aventurine.

**Planets:** The Sun/Jupiter.

**Element:** Fire.

**Sabbat:** Alban Hefin/Litha.

**Living things:** White horses, oriole and wren, mistletoe and coltsfoot.

The **oak,** a true forest king, most stately, long-lived and substantial of forest trees, is the embodiment of masculine power and virility, associated with ruler- and warrior Gods and with success, conquest and prosperity.

**Range:** The oak is found all over the Northern Hemisphere, particularly in North America, with about 500 species, many of which achieve great size and longevity. They are found across the Mediterranean region and down into North Africa, also in Australia and South America. The name "oak" is also used of semi-related and non-related species of trees.

The British oak species, *Q. robur* and *Q. petracea*, the common and sessile oaks, have long been planted in larger parks and in the grounds of stately homes, as well as in streets. They are easily recognised by their size, their mighty and rough trunks, their lobed leaves and the acorns which they produce in the summer and autumn. Oaks are deciduous, but some keep their leaves over the winter until the spring leaves are ready to emerge, like their cousin the beech.

Almost a third of the world's oak species are considered in danger of extinction, with *sudden oak death* a leading cause of loss of trees in the US, while the disease *acute oak decline* has been taking a toll in the UK since 2009.

Across Asia, the banyan tree, *Ficus benghalensis*, fills the role of the oak as a tree of kingship and majesty. The national tree of India, it has a Hindu festival associated with it and women petition the tree by tying threads around it for the health and safety of their husbands. The banyan is now also found in southern regions of the US. In China, a similar status is accorded to bamboo (*Bambusa vulgaris* and other spp), which represents nobility, integrity and a raft of associated virtues.

**Healing Properties:** The oak is quite poisonous and livestock should be kept from eating its leaves and nuts, with the exception of pigs, which thrive on acorns and were traditionally turned out into the forests to fatten on them by those foresters with rights of *pannage*. The high tannin content of the plant is what renders it toxic, but this component can also be used for healing as it is antibacterial and antiviral and can also be used as a vermifuge. The leaves can safely be used externally to treat inflammations and infections in external tissue and they have been used against venereal diseases in the past. Modern science has been investigating the oak for its anti-cancer qualities.

**Uses:** Mighty oaks once covered much of the UK but the depredations of monarchs, starting with Henry VIII building large naval fleets ("hearts of oak"), saw a vast acreage felled for timber over the centuries until metal ships became the norm in the nineteenth century. However, the oak remains the most common forest tree in the UK.

Oak, prized for its strength and lasting qualities, has been used for a huge number of things including timber-framed and lath-and-plaster houses, barns and sheds, staircases, flooring, doors, panelling, furniture, barrels, roofs – including impressive cathedral and church roofs – and veneers. The bark of the cork oak is used for bottle stoppers, notice boards, dart boards and floor tiles, and the oak galls (swellings on the branches caused by a parasitic insect) have been used in the manufacture of ink. The tannin-rich leaves are still used in the leather industry. The acorns can be rendered edible by soaking to remove much of the tannin, and can be ground into flour and roasted as a coffee substitute.

**Myth and Story:** Possibly the most iconic tree in the world, the oak is featured more than any other as a national, company or club emblem and appears in hundreds of folk tales. Examples of revered oaks are numerous, from the enormous oak in Sherwood Forest said to have been Robin Hood's centre of operations and the two gigantic hulks Gog and Magog at Glastonbury (one still just alive) to the 20-year-old oak sapling growing beside the original, felled Herne's Oak in Windsor Great Park – just some of many revered oak trees across the world. From the Royal Navy to the National Trust, many organisations use it as a badge and many people still observe the custom of wearing or carrying a sprig of oak on Oak Apple Day (29th May) to mark the restoration of the monarchy in 1660 and to remember the escape of the future King Charles II from the roundheads by hiding in an oak tree. King Arthur's round table is said to have been made from oak.

For some reason, perhaps its size and height, the oak is struck more often by lightning than other tree, and for this, amongst other reasons, it was most sacred to the Druids. They planted it in groves for their worship and probably derived their name "Druid" from the word for the oak, "duir", which also gives us our word "durable" and may be etymologically connected to "door" as well.

In modern paganism, the Oak King is seen as the embodiment of the waxing year, who surrenders his crown and his life to the Holly King as the year starts to wane after the summer solstice, but returns to his throne and power at the winter solstice, when days begin to lengthen.

Which children have not collected acorns and the little wooden cups they sit in, which were once believed to be used as drinking vessels by the fairies? They might also collect the little round galls, created by a wasp larva, which were often worn as good luck charms or used to foretell the weather for the coming year by cutting them open to see what was inside.

**Magic:** The twigs and leaves of oak are used in many spells, particularly to invoke masculine power and the God, or in prosperity magic. As with many protective trees, you can bind two oak twigs into an equal-armed cross with a piece of red cord or thread and hang it in the window or doorway to protect the home from misfortune. Some people carry an acorn as a good luck charm, as it will give you the powers of the oak: youthfulness, long life and strength; and the little galls or "oak apples" can also be threaded onto a cord and worn for good luck and protection. The acorn protects against lightning.

**Divination:** The Ogham *few* Duir speaks of success and achievement, of a person climbing the ladder of their life, filled with inner strength and confidence, determined to achieve what they have set out to do. It can be about financial success, about money and riches and rising in one's career, or of being voted or elevated into a higher position. It can speak of people or organisations of power, such as armies, governments, the law or financial institutions or simply powerful groups of any kind. It can also speak of physical strength and of good health and of renewal and rest. It is a lucky *few* to draw.

**Reversed:** It speaks of powerlessness, of failure, of falling short, of disappointments.

## *Visualisation Story*

The woodland is silent and cold, rime gleaming on the branches and twigs and a light dusting of snow around the roots of the trees, just being touched by the growing light in the east. The Sun has not yet shown above the horizon but the wood is hushed and expectant, awaiting the first narrow rim of gold to appear.

An army of people, all dressed in green or in white Druids' robes, suddenly come pouring along the woodland path, their faces bright with happiness and anticipation. Many of them also wear headdresses or wreaths made of ivy or other evergreen leaves from the trees around them or carry branches in their hands. Some are singing, some banging drums or playing panpipes. There are children among them too, many carrying nuts and fruit.

At last, they reach a large clearing in the woods, just lit with the horizontal rays that are growing by the minute in the east. On the north side of the clearing is a massive oak tree, clearly centuries old but upright and stately, its bare branches lifted to the sky in majesty.

Here the procession halts, their eyes on the horizon visible through the trees to one side of the great oak. The singing and music die away and a deep hush falls on the company; even the children are quiet, realising something is about to happen. Slowly, slowly, the first glowing red crescent of the Sun lifts above the horizon: it is Midwinter's Day. A hushed murmur grows in the crowd of people, children giggle.

When they grow quiet again, they turn towards the great oak tree to see two men are now standing under its immense branches. They are brothers, it seems, for they look very alike, although the older seems tired, bowed with age, even unwell.

The younger man embraces his brother, who seems to take strength from this closeness and stands a little straighter, even appears to look a little younger.

"You are tired, brother," says the younger one, who is a tall, noble man with a kingly aspect, completely untouched by age. He is still, standing facing his brother, his hands on the other's shoulders in a loving manner. "You have worked and striven, borne the load, and now it is time for you to let go."

The older man's face gladdens and he raises his hands to his head. He is wearing a withered wreath of twigs and dead brown holly leaves, almost invisible amongst his greying hair, and he now lifts this off and places it on his brother's head. As the crowd watch, holding their breath, the leaves of the wreath quiver, then change colour, lifting, brightening and growing into vibrant green oak leaves. As they watch, the Sun rises fully above the horizon, flooding the clearing with golden light and shining full on the Oak King.

The Holly King returns to the crowd, already looking refreshed and younger, his steps stronger and his back straighter. The Oak King stands under the oak, his gaze sombre but filled with determination and courage.

## Tinne ░ Challenge, Struggle, Fight for Right.

Corresponds to our letter T.
Pronounced CHIN-yuh.
**Tree:** The holly: *Ilex aquifolium*.
**Male**
**Rune:** Teiwaz or Uruz
**Tarot:** Strength
**Qabalah:** Teth, the 19th path.
**Deity(ies):** Jupiter/Zeus, Lugh, Mars, Saturn, Taranis, Thor.
**Correspondences:** Colour: red. Crystals: ruby and bloodstone.
**Planets:** Mars and Saturn.

**Element:** Fire.
**Sabbat:** Lughnasadh/Lammas.
**Living Things:** Cardinal, starling, meadowsweet.

**Holly** is a handsome tree whose rich glossy green leaves, armed with vicious spines, stay on the tree all year round, complimented in winter by the scarlet berries. It has been used by many cultures to which it is native to decorate the home over the winter season and its festivals.

**Range:** *Ilex aquifolium*, a slow-growing tree which does not achieve a great height and does not bear fruit until it is around 40 years old, is found across most of Europe, growing in all soil types in open woodlands and hedgerows. The tree is often grown in parks and larger gardens for its evergreen and decorative qualities, and hollies with variegated leaves and different coloured berries have been developed. Other related species, not all of which are evergreen, are found more or less all over the world, including the tropics and sub-tropics. Strange as this may seem to the British, the Ilex genus is so large that it has members in all the types of climate in the world and Europe is the poorest of these, with only the one species occurring naturally – our familiar Christmas holly.

**Healing Properties:** While the berries and leaves of the European holly are toxic, some species of holly have been used to make tea, and the bark can be used in infusions to break a fever, while the leaves have been used against urinary tract infections. Culpeper recommended a poultice of holly bark on broken or dislocated bones.

**Uses:** Holly wood is liable to split, and therefore not used for building or furniture, but it is hard and dense and small turned items are made from it such as handles and small tools, also billiard cues! The attractively coloured wood also makes beautiful wands. The berries are very poisonous, though many birds eat them with impunity. In the past, the prickly leaves were pushed into corners and mouse-holes to deter vermin and even pushed down mole tunnels to prevent mole damage to lawns. The leaves were boiled and used to make birdlime. Interestingly, the tree bears thorny leaves only on its lower branches and does not bother to arm the leaves that are beyond the reach of grazing animals. Some farmers grow common holly for the Christmas market, when there is a huge demand.

**Myth and Story:** The holly is deeply rooted in Christian culture where it became associated with Christ's Crown of Thorns and its berries with his blood. It is especially connected to Christmas, starring in the lyrics of many carols and emblazoned across greeting cards and wrapping paper. Before Christianity the pagan Norsemen brought it inside at midwinter to decorate the home with its shiny leaves and bright red berries. In modern pagan belief it calls to mind the story of the Oak King and Holly King, often enacted at midsummer and midwinter, as these two halves of the pagan God battle for prominence, one beating the other as the year turns. The Holly King is the God of the dying year and takes over from his summer brother at either midsummer or harvest. Like several other figures in folklore, the Holly King wields a holly club.

Very sacred to the Druids, who saw it as second only to the oak and decorated their homes with evergreens in winter to provide a sanctuary for nature spirits, the holly was seen as protective by the Celts, who would plant it close to a house to keep away evil spirits and bad luck. Despite its own poisonous content, it was supposed to protect against poisoning, as well as lightning strikes and evil magic. If holly with berries is brought into the house at Christmas/Yule there will be good luck for each berry on the boughs but if any fall, the luck will be diminished.

**Magic:** Hollies are very protective, as seen when planted near the house (very old specimens are sometimes seen planted right against the door of old houses and inns) or in the use of their leaves and wands made from their wood in protective magic. The country folk of old believed it protected their homes from lightning strikes and it is thus associated with thunder deities like Thor and Taranis. The leaves can be placed at the threshold to repel bad spirits, perhaps under the doormat. The tree and its parts are also lucky and can be carried like a charm to attract good luck, and are also used in work for psychic enhancement. Its protective qualities can be used at harvest time or planting season to protect the crops for the coming year.

**Divination:** Tinne is the Ogham *few* of the warrior and speaks of a challenge or a struggle to which you will bring not only your own sense of right and justice, but your experience, your knowledge and your valour. Trust your instincts and wield your weapon with determination and confidence but without excess aggression. Remember: courage itself can put enemies to flight without a weapon being raised. Your courage and your trust in yourself protect you. The *few* also speaks of creative abilities and natural talents, your ability to deal with the world, as well as your ability to create beautiful artwork!

**Reversed:** The *few* speaks of hardships, of situations perhaps beyond your ability to cope. You must draw back and rethink your strategies.

## *Visualisation Story*

A group of eco-protesters have gathered at a meeting being attended by local councillors and other dignitaries, to protest the destruction of some ancient woodland, home to dormice, badgers and two species of rare butterflies. The site is scheduled to become yet another housing estate to make profits for a huge development company with which, it is suspected, the local MP has some secret ties.

A large car draws up and the MP gets out, brushing down his expensive suit and smoothing his hair. He looks at the crowd and their placards and smirks very slightly. Then he turns and moves to enter the building.

A woman comes forward from the crowd. She is not like many of the others: small, elderly and quiet seeming, she is wearing unexciting Marks & Spencer's clothing and has a tidy but rather dated hairstyle. She is not waving a placard or chanting. Because she looks a little different and non-aggressive, the MP pauses as she approaches him.

"Yes?" he asks, putting on his for-the-camera smile.

The woman stops in front of him and just looks at him for a long moment, so that he begins to turn away, thinking she has nothing to say. This is when she speaks.

"I just wanted to look at you," she says, "I just wanted to see what kind of a person would allow this, just for money you don't even need. Allow the destruction of something unique and precious, something that can never be replaced. Your name will go down as someone who stood by and let it happen, encouraged it even."

She does not sound violent or even rancorous, just calm, resigned and a little contemptuous, and something about her, her expression, her tone of voice, perhaps her very ordinariness, seems to stop him in his tracks. He opens his mouth to speak, but nothing comes out. After a second, he backs away, finds some platitude to call to the crowd who are now pressing close. The woman stands still in a little circle of space, still looking directly at him. Her expression does not change. He turns and almost runs into the council offices.

Hours later, the press has joined the protesters and are there to hear that the development plan has been thrown out. The MP is smiling like a crocodile, telling anyone who will listen that he knows his responsibilities to the environment as well as his constituents, that he was personally responsible for the decision. His eyes flicker over the crowd, but the woman is no longer there.

## *Coll ᚉ Inspiration, Wisdom, Knowledge.*

ᚉ

Corresponds to our letter C, as in *cat*.
Pronounced CULL.
**Tree:** The hazel: *Corylus avellana*.
**Male or sometimes both genders**
**Rune:** Kenaz.
**Tarot:** The Magician.
**Qabalah:** Beth, the 12th path.
**Deity(ies):** Athena/Minerva, Bride, Hermes/Mercury, Ogma, Thor, Thoth, all deities of inspiration, wisdom and knowledge.
**Correspondences:** Colours: orange and dark blue. Crystals: topaz and pearl.
**Planets:** Mercury and the Sun.
**Element:** Air.
**Sabbat:** Lughnasadh.
**Living Things:** Crane, salmon, vervain.

**Hazel's** name comes from the Anglo-Saxon word *haezl*, meaning a headdress or wreath formed from flexible hazel twigs – many pagans to this day make their basic wreaths from hazel withies collected from the hedgerow, to be garnished later with flowers, leaves and other materials appropriate to the festival about to be celebrated. Crowning the head, the hazel is also of the mind, the tree of inspiration and enlightenment.

**Range:** The 18 Corylus species are found across Europe, North America, Asia, parts of the Mediterranean and North Africa, growing in woodlands, hedgerows, parks and gardens – ornamental forms of hazel have been developed, including the purple hazel (*Corylus maxima purpurea*) and the contorted hazel (*Corylus avellana contorta*). The tree, easily identified from its large bright green leaves, which are round but toothed, has a low-growing habit, usually with several trunks rather than one – which may indicate it has been coppiced. Most world mythologies have a tree they associate with inspiration, knowledge and spiritual insights – famously, in India, the Bodhi tree under which the Buddha received nirvana, the Ficus religiosa.

**Healing Properties:** The hazel has very few healing properties, although the ancient Greek physician, Pliny, recommended a tea made from the crushed nuts as a remedy for a persistent cough, and Culpeper suggested a poultice of warm nuts and shells for painful joints. Including it in the diet has significant health benefits, as it is nutritionally rich, with proteins, healthy fats, fibre and a range of micronutrients.

**Uses:** Hazel has been a crop for mankind since earliest times, with the nuts being harvested on an industrial scale for food in the UK until the twentieth century. They are still grown here today on a smaller scale, notably in Kent, although most of the hazelnuts you will find in the supermarket are now imported. The nuts have a delicious flavour and are used in the manufacture of confectionery, cakes, oils, liqueurs, nut butters and spreads, vegetarian foods and breakfast cereals.

Hazel wood is extremely flexible and has been used down the ages for baskets and hurdles. Hazel staves were used in the infilling of wall sections in Mediaeval lath-and-plaster houses, when they would be plastered over with mud and lime plaster to create a solid wall which has in many cases lasted for centuries with no more maintenance than the odd coat of paint. They are also still used as thatching spars and in furniture. Gardeners are again using hazel sticks as a more ecologically-friendly alternative to imported bamboo pea- and bean-sticks.

**Myth and Story:** Nuts have been associated with knowledge and wisdom in many cultures and in Celtic legend they grew over the Well of Wisdom, where salmon swam. The fish ate the nuts as they fell into the water, and thereby absorbed their magical inspiration. Anyone who ate the salmon would also take in this magical gift – in one story, Fionn Mac Cumhall, the Irish hero, gained this by accident when young. Instructed by his Druid master to prepare one of the magical salmon for him, Fionn touched the fish and its juice splashed on his hand. At once, he put his hand to his mouth to suck the burn and the magical wisdom passed into him (note the similarity of this to the legend of Cerridwen and Taliessin).

The Norsemen called hazel the "Tree of Wisdom" and held it as sacred to Thor. The Romans saw it as a tree of peace and men might carry a branch to a meeting for negotiation between warring enemies, as they might carry a white flag in later times. It is also said to have the power to repel snakes.

**Magic:** Inspiration is important to the Druids, who revere this tree for its magical association with wisdom and knowledge and use hazel wands and staffs in ritual to gain these qualities. The tree is protective and will shield a house from lightning strikes.

Our ancestors believed so thoroughly in its divinatory powers that they trusted they could establish the guilt or innocence of someone accused of a serious crime, such as murder, by using a forked hazel rod in the same way as a water diviner.

**Divination:** The best-known use of hazel in this context is for water divining, a practice which has come out of the broom closet and achieved acceptance among landowners, farmers, builders and others generally assumed to be more "hard-headed" than modern pagan practitioners. Wendy knows a farmer, a man of some substance, who does his own water divining, yet has no belief in magic or superstition. The classic hazel divining rod is a Y-shaped branch which is held lightly between the fingers by the forked end, with the single tine hanging free. When it feels water underneath, whether an underground stream or even water or sewer pipes, the rod will move in a certain way in the holder's hands. Divination in this manner can also be used to find things other than water, such as buried treasure, lost possessions, paths and hidden things.

The Ogham *few* speaks of inspiration, particularly poetic inspiration, and knowledge gained through work or by magic, of wishes and good fortune, prosperity and fertility, of finding things hidden or lost. It speaks of the realm of the mind and the spirit, of the brain (both the right and left hemispheres), of poetry, art and music, and of skills, knowledge and science.

**Reversed:** It will have the opposite meaning and speak of an inability to see or find out, of things being hidden, lost or unobtainable, of being misled and getting nowhere, of ignorance and misinformation.

## Visualisation Story

You are strolling through open woodland. Where sunlight penetrates through to the woodland floor; green plants and colourful wildflowers bloom on all sides. Birdsong fills the air, butterflies flutter in the rays of sunlight that come through the tree canopy and there is a fresh sweet smell of blossom and green things. As you walk, the nature of the woods changes a little, the path broadens and the trees grow smaller, until you realise you are walking through gardens rather than wild land, where the trees and bushes have been chosen for their coloured leaves and attractive flowers and pruned and shaped. The path goes on, becoming straighter now. At last it leads you to an enclosure within the gardens where tall trees lean over the low stone wall of a broad well. The trees are hazels, and as you watch, one drops a nut into the water and a large silvery fish rises to the surface and swallows it, with a musical *plunk*.

You come closer to the water's edge and look down. There are many of the large silver fish gliding in the water, but you notice that there is something different about them. They are salmon, very large and beautiful, but there is something about their faces that draws your attention, though you cannot put your finger on the reason. Now and then, one of them rises to the surface and looks hard at you. The look they give you is nothing like the aimless look of any fish you have ever seen; it is purposeful, intelligent and full of meaning. It is so strange to see this human expression on the face of a fish that you sit down on the stony wall of the well and stare at them.

One by one the fish rise up and stare at you, and one by one they sink again and swim away. You sense that they are conferring about you, but that they are not yet decided what to do about you. Patiently you wait, sure that something is going to happen, that there is some message or sign for you here.

Slowly, slowly, a dark grey shape begins to rise from the depths. It gets larger and its colour lightens to silver and shines brighter as it comes, until the most enormous freshwater fish you have ever seen has come to the surface. It seems ancient beyond belief, with ragged fins and weeds growing from its scales, yet its eyes are those of a person; there is no doubt that this is a supremely wise being who has seen centuries pass and monarchs and governments rise and fall.

You lean low over the water, bowing respectfully to this god among fish. Then he speaks. What he says to you is a piece of wisdom you were told by someone wise, long ago – something you have always clung to, and by which you have lived your life. What this ancient fish is telling you is that you were right, and now he tells you one more thing: a piece of advice you will always cherish, and which will shape your behaviour forever.

Thank the fish and come away from the well; it has given you what you needed.

## Quert or Ceirt ⏐⏐⏐⏐ Healing, love, Choice.

Corresponds to our letters Qu, as in *queen*.
Pronounced QUAIRT.
**Tree:** The apple tree: *Malus domestica* or *Malus sylvestris, Malus spp.*
**Female**
**Rune:** Ingwaz.
**Tarot:** The Lovers.
**Qabalah:** Zayin, the 17th path.
**Deity(ies):** Aengus, Demeter, Freyja and Frigga, Hera/Juno, Iduna, Pomona.
**Correspondences:** Colours: pink and light green. Crystals: emerald and rose quartz.
**Planet:** Venus.
**Element:** Water.
**Sabbat:** Alban Elfed/Mabon and Samhain/Samhuinn.
**Living Things:** Butterflies, lilies, lovebirds.

Perhaps the most domesticated of all trees, the **apple** has been a welcome addition to cottage gardens for thousands of years. Even before refrigeration, its fruit was enjoyed for most of the year as it is possible, with care, to store apples over the winter.

**Range:** Apples are believed to have originated in Central Asia and to have spread along the Silk Route into Europe. They were introduced to Britain by the Romans. In American history, they were spread across the continent by the generosity of "Johnny Appleseed" – a real-life nurseryman who gave away seeds and saplings to all and sundry. Today the apple and its close relative the pear are grown across the world and are important both commercially and culturally. The tree is typically small, achieving no more than about 20 feet in height, and not especially long-lived either. It is commonly grown in back gardens for its fruit, where it may be grown in a decorative and more accessible espaliered form, and in orchards, but many decorative varieties have been developed which are grown in parks and gardens. The wild variety found in Europe and the US is known as "crab apple" and may even have thorns.

Another tree which has very similar associations is the myrtle, native to the Mediterranean and Asia, which is sacred to Juno/Hera and believed to bring good fortune to couples getting married. It is a traditional part of the bride's bouquet in some regions. The tamarisk tree is associated in some countries with love and marriage and with health, and so is the walnut, because of its nut being composed of two tightly-packed halves.

**Healing Properties:** The fruit has intrinsic healing qualities and is certainly a healthful addition to the human diet. In past ages, winter-stored apples would have been the main if not only source of vitamin C and they are also rich in fibre. Apples have a beneficial effect on the gut and its vital natural bacteria. The phytochemicals found in the skin and pips are under investigation by modern science for their potential as medicine. Apples contain fisetin – the most powerful of all the flavonoids – so maybe the Norsemen were onto something with their legend of Iduna, who kept the Gods young with her magic apples. Largely water and fibre, with a range of micronutrients, they have a range of health benefits, including lowering cholesterol and boosting the immune system.

The apple can also be used in magical healing, due to its ancient associations. For example, the old wisewoman's cure for warts, which was to cut an apple through the centre so the pentagram showed, rub it on the wart and then bury it in the ground so the wart would decay and disappear.

**Uses:** Although the tree is small and the timber therefore not used for large projects, the attractive, hard wood has been used for a range of things; principally furniture and turned items such as handles, kitchen tools and veneers. Because of its hardness it is used for mallet heads. It is also much-prized as a firewood as, when burned, it gives off a very pleasant aroma. The fruit are popular across the world and around 7,500 different varieties of apples have been developed, from huge cooking apples like the traditional Bramley to small, sweet "eating apples" like Cox's Orange Pippin. The science of grafting has even made it possible to grow trees that bear more than one variety of apple. They are eaten fresh or turned into baked goods such as pies, tarts and the old-fashioned dessert called apple dumplings, or dried and added to cereal mixes. They are made into apple sauce, apple butter and apple cheese, may be added to jams made with other fruit (for their pectin which sets the jam) and also made into cider and cider vinegar, cordial, juices and wines, spirituous liquors and even coated with toffee as the well-loved childhood treat "toffee apples". Apple blossom is also used in the manufacture of perfume and toiletries.

**Myth and Story:** Apples are found in mythologies, folk tales and stories all over the world, from the Bible to CS Lewis's *Narnia* stories, often as a symbolic fruit which should not be taken. In Classical mythology, the apple became a symbol of choice or judgement in the legend of Paris, who was asked to judge who was the most beautiful Goddess between Hera, Athena and Aphrodite (he chose Aphrodite, who promised him the most beautiful woman in the world – Helen of Troy – thus provoking the Trojan Wars). Herakles stole the Golden Apples of the Hesperides as one of his Twelve Labours. The Greek Goddess and heroine, Atalanta, lost a running race and was forced to marry because she could not stop herself picking up golden apples thrown in her path by Hippomenes, who wanted to marry her.

In Celtic belief, the apple tree and its fruit were a symbol of rebirth and regeneration and its fruits were buried with the dead to give them nourishment on their journey to the afterlife. King Arthur was spirited away to Avalon (Isle of Apples) by the witch or fairy Morgan after he was mortally wounded at Camlann. The silver bough or branch turns up in Celtic mythology as a magical gift with strings: when the hero Bran is lured by it to a mysterious "Land of Women" – he finds when he returns that, Rip Van Winkle-like, he has been away for centuries.

The Norse Gods are kept alive and youthful by the apples growing in Iduna's magic orchard and when they are stolen, the Gods start to age, so steps are taken to get them back (Loki being responsible for this mischief, as usual!).

Wassailing – the tradition of blessing and encouraging the trees – is still done today around Yule, with people toasting the trees with cider, pouring cider at their roots and performing other ritual actions to protect the orchard and ensure a good harvest for the following year. Other traditions associated with apples include ducking for them in a barrel of water.

To modern pagans, the apple is considered a magical fruit because of its historical associations and because of the pentagram found within the fruit if it is cut in cross section between the stalk and blossom ends, formed of the seeds and their hard ovules, and it has become deeply associated with the Sabbat Alban Elfed or Mabon, the Second Harvest, as well as with Samhuinn/Samhain.

**Magic:** Apples and their pips have been used in love charms for many centuries. Apple blossom is an ingredient of love spells, especially when combined with other "rosy" items, such as rose incense, rose quartz crystals and pink candles. The protection of apple is that of the health.

**Divination:** Apples have been used for romantic divination for centuries, including the practice of peeling an apple in one piece at Samhain and throwing the peel over one's shoulder. The peel is said to form the initial of the person you will marry, but if it breaks you will stay unmarried!

Whilst in Christian mythology the apple seems to be connected with sin, loss of innocence and knowledge gained through wrong means, in other cultures it has always been a symbol of health, success, love and achievement, and also of favour: remember Paris awarding the Golden Apple to Aphrodite, judging her the fairest Goddess, and the traditional "apple for the teacher" brought by schoolchildren hoping for "Miss's" approval. The Ogham *few* Quert speaks of both health and love, and also rejuvenation and longevity. Drawing this Ogham letter tells you that your health and vitality are or will be good, or it can be a hint to take extra care of them to ensure that they are.

**Reversed:** This can indicate a problem with your health or a disappointment in love or with your relationship.

## *Visualisation Story*

You are standing on a stony path which goes down a hillside and up the other side, finally approaching a fair city, which gleams in the Sun as though the roofs are all of gold. The Sun is rising in the east and birdsong is in the air. There is dew on the grass and leaves and on the intricate spiders' webs that adorn the trees. You see these things, but you do not appreciate them as you should, for you are feeling quite unwell – a bad cold, or perhaps something more serious that you have become aware of recently.

A fair woman carrying a basket appears on the path leading from the golden city and moving so quickly that she covers the distance in a much shorter time than you expect and is soon walking past you. She is so beautiful that you can almost not look at her directly, and you soon begin to realise that She is a Goddess. She enters the ornate gate of a walled orchard, leaving it open so that you are able to follow and, as you are now filled with curiosity, you do so. She takes no notice of you, but moves purposely among the trees, which are loaded with the most enormous apples you have ever seen, each one being a shining golden colour instead of the usual green or red of common apples. Slowly She fills the basket, pausing at each tree and carefully scrutinising each fruit. Some She takes, others She passes over, and as She picks a fruit, She murmurs a name – a different name for each apple. One particular fruit, a brighter gold than the others, She picks and smells, and then places a kiss on the shining skin, murmuring "Bragi" – the name of Her divine husband.

At last, Her work of fruit picking is over, Her basket is filled with beautiful fruit and She turns to leave the orchard. You cough, still feeling unwell, or perhaps give some other sign of your affliction. Iduna turns towards you. She feels sympathy for you, it is clear, but She must be on Her way to Asgard and the Gods who need Her magic apples to keep them well and strong. She hesitates, then picks a small apple from the nearest tree and holds it out to you.

"One bite only," She cautions, and watches to make sure you do not take more. The apple tastes better than anything you have ever eaten; sweet, winey and filled with a power that seems to flow through you as though you had been given alcohol. Your symptoms disappear at once and you feel as well as you ever have, and better.

You fall on your knees and thank Iduna, but She is holding open the gate for you, impatient to be about Her duties, so you thank Her and hurry out of the orchard. Iduna locks the gate and is off, walking slowly – yet faster than a horse can run – towards the city.

## AICME 3

### Muin ┼ Truth and Prophecy, Harvest, Celebration.

Corresponds to our letter M.

Pronounced MUHN.

**Tree:** The grapevine: *Vitis vinifera* or, we suggest the bramble: *Rubus fruticosus*.

**Male and Female** (vine), **Female** (bramble).

**Rune:** Fehu, Jera, Wunjo.

**Tarot:** Temperance.

**Qabalah:** Samekh, the 25th path.

**Deity(ies):** Bast, Bacchus, Demeter, Dionysus, the Fae, Hathor, Silenus.

**Correspondences:** Colours: all colours (vine), pink and white (bramble). Crystal: emerald.

**Planets:** The Moon (vine), Venus (bramble).

**Element:** Air.

**Sabbat:** The harvest Sabbats Lughnasadh and Alban Elfed/ Mabon.

**Living Things:** Swans, lizards, titmouse.

The **Vine** is another of those plants like holly which produces an immediate response in the mind to the sight of its leaves and tendrils: in this case harvest and wellbeing. The sheer bounty of the ripe fruit hanging in glistening bunches has made it a popular addition to dinner tables for special occasions everywhere. It speaks of feasting, of celebration, of bounty and of everything that is mentioned in Keats' iconic poem, *Ode to Autumn*.

The **Bramble** has all these associations and more; while it is certainly a beautiful and tempting sight with its pretty pale pink blossoms, followed by fat, shining fruits hanging in enormous quantities; it has always had a shadier side, through its association with the Fae in British belief. Unlike the grape, it is also armed with thorns, making the gathering of the fruit rather more difficult than the snipping away of a bunch of grapes.

**Range:** Originating in the Mediterranean region, vines grow almost everywhere in warmer climates and even in temperate regions like the UK, where vineyards have sprung up in many southern areas since the Romans brought them here as early as 43CE. Bramble species grow across Europe, the Americas, North Africa and Asia. So, between them, these two plants have got the world pretty well covered. Blackberry hybrids have been developed both for commercial use and for gardens, including thornless varieties.

**Healing Properties:** Grapes and blackberries are both stuffed with beneficial vitamins, particularly vitamin C. In the case of grapes, the wine has been made into spirituous liquors like brandy, which is known for restoring a person who feels faint or unwell. Grapes also contain resveratrol – a powerful anti-inflammatory and antioxidant which is believed to fight cancers, heart disease and diabetes. They are also rich in potassium, which lowers blood pressure and maintains heart health. Both types of fruit also contain flavonoids and dietary fibre, and blackberries have vitamins A and K and also calcium and Omega-3. The Greeks valued brambles for healing, believing they had the power to cure snake bites, mouth ulcers, bleeding gums and loosening teeth (their natural vitamin C content would certainly help with this). Brambles have a habit of arching over and rooting their tips in the soil and in the past people would pass sick children through such an arch, believing it would heal them.

**Uses:** Grape vines are associated primarily with the pleasures of the table, principally the production of wine and its by-products, stronger distilled alcoholic drinks such as brandy; although the fruit is also eaten fresh or dried, as sultanas and raisins, which are also baked into cakes and confectionary. The leaves are also eaten and you can buy them in jars of brine at your local supermarket to make dolmades (stuffed vine leaves), a traditional Greek dish. The tendrils have also been used in weaving to make baskets and other items.

At the top of the "food-for-free" list, blackberries are prized everywhere they grow for their delicious sweetness and versatility and made into puddings, jams, jellies, cordials and country wines. Though they are grown commercially, blackberrying is often seen as an occasion for a traditional family outing to the countryside, returning home with baskets of fruit to enjoy.

**Myth and Story:** One of the very earliest cultivated fruiting plants, the grape vine is deeply associated in Classical myth with fertility Gods, particularly Bacchus and Dionysus, who are often depicted wearing wreaths of grapes and vine leaves on their heads. Dionysus also has a rather comical drunken old companion called Silenus, his guardian and tutor, who oversees grape production and winemaking. The grief-stricken Dionysus turned his lover Ampelos into a grapevine after he was slain by a wild bull. In ancient Egypt, the people honoured the fertility Goddesses Hathor and Bast with a "Day of Drunkenness." Grapes have always been associated with harvest bounty, celebration and merry-making; from the orgiastic festivals of history to the elegant flutes of champagne served at weddings today.

In some cultures the eating of blackberries is taboo, as they are seen as belonging to the Fae. In Christian culture, blackberries are seen as undesirable after Michaelmas (29th September) as on that date the Devil drags his tail over them (or in some versions urinates on them!). The Greeks valued them, believing they came from blood shed by the Titans in their war with the Gods, and that they had healing powers. Modern pagans associate them with Alban Elfed/Mabon and often serve desserts made with them at this festival.

Blackberries are also seen as symbolic of neglect and abandonment, as in the fairytale *Sleeping Beauty*, where they grow all over the castle where she and her family and servants lie asleep for a hundred years, hiding it from sight. In any garden that is not tended regularly, they certainly do take hold very quickly.

**Magic:** Wine has always been used in ritual, and is still part of the Christian communion ritual today, while modern pagans use it in the "cakes and wine" part of a ritual as it comes to an end, to ground and share. The ancients in many cultures used wine as part of a sacrifice to the Gods and modern pagans will also pour some on the earth or into a libation bowl at the end of a ceremony. All the Ogham trees are considered protective, but vines and blackberries are typically associated with protection of the home and property. Just as blackberries – or even tough old vines – might form a barrier to intruders bent on mischief, so these symbols can also be used to keep one's home and land safe.

Grapes and vines can be used in fertility magic, especially in the garden. A piece of blackberry vine, stripped of its thorns, can be carried as an amulet against misfortune.

**Divination:** In the case of the vine, one of the main meanings of this *few* is truth-telling, perhaps because people who have taken drink tend to blurt out the truth despite themselves (*in vino veritas!*). But of course, blackberries are also made into wine, so this meaning can also be attached to the bramble. In ancient cultures, alcohol was sometimes used to alter consciousness for the purpose of prophecy, and this is another meaning of this *few*.

Grapes and blackberries start to ripen around the same time in late summer and are associated with harvest and the reaping of good things, just so does this *few* speak of personal harvests and achievements, of long term plans come to good, of benefits won through hard work. One of the things we associate with the harvest is a good old knees-up – a celebration, with plenty to eat and drink; so this *few* can also speak of a celebration of some kind, perhaps a wedding after a long engagement, when the couple have spent years saving up for their special day, or the "harvest" of a newborn baby and the party that might be held to welcome him into the family at a wiccaning or christening. Perhaps a promotion is indicated, after a long time serving an apprenticeship or learning a new job, or the ability, after much scrimping, saving and working overtime, to buy a new car … or a home.

**Reversed:** Lies, deceit, misinformation, disappointment and the opposite of all the foregoing is indicated by the reversed symbol.

## *Visualisation Story*

A barn is decked out for a feast, with trestle tables laid with clean, white cloths and plates, cups and cutlery, while the floor is swept clean of straw and dirt and the beams overhead are decorated with swags of hops, flowers and greenery.

As you watch, a procession comes in sight, winding its way through the fields; men, women and children, many crowned with wreaths of greenery and flowers, some of the younger men pulling a rough cart. They come into the farmyard, laughing and talking, and you get a closer view of the cart. A rough throne made from straw bales covered in cloth is set up in its centre and on it sits a pretty young girl, clearly representing a Goddess of fertility or crops, dressed in a white dress and wearing a headdress of barley, flowers and leaves. She is surrounded by bounty, by sheaves of corn, gourds, baskets of fruit and flowers, and two girls dressed in pretty dresses sit in the cart with her as attendants. The cart is towed into the barn and pushed to the far end, where a rough stage has been erected from straw bales and planks. Some of the men help the young Goddess out of the cart and lift her gently on to the stage where she takes her seat on a rough-hewn wooden throne, with her attendants sitting on either side of her. Others take the harvest offerings of fruit, vegetables, flowers and corn from the cart and assemble them around the stage. The crowd gather round and sing a merry song to celebrate the harvest and praise the Goddess who has brought them such good fortune. Meanwhile, women from the farmhouse are bringing in great platters of meat, cheeses, bread, pasties, pies and vegetables, and laying them on the tables. Others bring in brimming jugs of cider and beer. Some musicians set up in a corner and start to play merry folk songs, some a little crude, which provokes gales of laughter from the adults in the barn who have now seated themselves eagerly at the tables and are helping themselves to the fare. More drink is brought, including some country wines in ancient, corked bottles, and soon the company are more than merry and the noise of singing and laughter from the barn spills out into the silent evening fields.

## Gort ╫ Friendship and Loyalty.

Corresponds to our letter G, as in *gate*.
Pronounced GORT.
**Tree:** The ivy: *Hedera helix.*
**Female**
**Rune:** Mannaz
**Tarot:** The Sun.
**Qabalah:** Resh, the 30th path.
**Deity(ies):** Bacchus, Bran,Dionysus, Osiris, Saturn.
**Correspondences:** Colours: blue and light brown. Crystal: azurite.
**Planet:** Saturn.
**Element:** Water.
**Sabbat:** Yule.
**Living Things:** Swan, lark, swallow, butterflies, woody nightshade.

Most decorative of climbing plants with its striking glossy leaves, the **ivy** is well endowed with associations. Since Victorian times, when flower names were fashionable, it has been given as a first name to girls. Its climbing, twining habit has become associated with age, as in the old trees round which it grows; and in America with academia, as in *Ivy League*, referring to the older universities whose venerable buildings might be clad with this plant. Its evergreen leaves have also become part of the imagery associated with Christmas in Christian culture.

**Range:** The 12-15 species of ivies are found across the whole of Europe, America, North Africa and Asia, but the name "ivy" has also become used for non-related species of vines across the world which climb trees and buildings.

**Healing Properties:** Ivy leaves were once stewed and the liquor used as a balm for skin rashes and ulcers, while the ground leaves might be used as a poultice on swellings. It has been used against coughs, including whooping cough, bronchitis and asthma, and may have anti-cancer properties. It is antibacterial and anti-inflammatory, and also detoxifies the body. Ivy extract helps the circulation and studies have shown it is beneficial to arthritis sufferers and can kill breast cancer cells. The berries, however, are slightly poisonous and the leaves may cause problems when in contact with the skin.

**Uses:** While the ivy does not have many uses outside horticulture, it has always been extremely popular as a garden plant and as a houseplant and many varieties have been developed with variegated foliage and attractively shaped leaves. It is valued as a climber and used to hide unattractive outbuildings, walls and fences. The yellow pom-pom flowers attract and feed many insects, including bees and butterflies. Because it is evergreen, ivy has been adopted, with holly, as one of the emblems of Christmas and brought into the house as a decoration.

**Myth and Story:** Like all the plants chosen for the Ogham, ivy was considered protective and it had a special connection to strong drink: the leaves, bruised or heated in wine, were taken to alleviate a hangover, and the ancients even believed wearing ivy leaves in a wreath on your head could prevent you from getting drunk. Bacchus is often shown wearing ivy leaves, as well as vine leaves. Ivy was also hung or grown above dairies and cowsheds to protect livestock and their produce.

**Magic:** Ivy can be used for any magic around love and friendship, perhaps to keep a lover true or to strengthen the bonds between a couple. In the past a clergyman marrying a couple might have presented them with a little bouquet of ivy; placed on the altar this plant can bring these energies into the working. Its clockwise spiral growth habit speaks of earth energies and can be used to encourage these in any magical working that draws them up.

**Divination:** The twining, embracing habit of ivy has always caused it to be associated with friendship, steadfastness, tenacity and loyalty, and the *few* speaks of your friends, your family, your circle of support. There is no need to be alone, nor is this the time to suffer by yourself, says the symbol. Turn to friends and know that, as you have been a good friend to them, so they will be there for you. Now is the time for loyalty and support, whether that means giving this to someone else or needing it from another. Open yourself to friendship, for much strength lies in the love and loyalty of others.

**Reversed:** The *few* can mean you are without this support and warns of loneliness and the bitter ordeal of struggling on by yourself through a difficult situation. It can indicate bad or toxic friends from whom you should distance yourself.

## Visualisation Story

Jess and Emily are at university and share a room. They have been best friends since they were very young and even applied to the same universities so that they would not have to be parted. Many of their classes are the same and their spare time is spent together, studying or enjoying the night life.

One afternoon Jess is checking her laptop to see it is charged when there is a knock at the door. She is expecting Emily back from her lunch date with her boyfriend, so merely calls, "Come in – s'open!"

Mark puts his head around the door and passes her a note. Jess leaves it on the shelf by the door and gets on with what she is doing, preparing for her afternoon class, and it is not until sometime later that she remembers the note and goes to read it. When she does, she sits down suddenly in a chair, her eyes wide and her breathing fast. Before she can stop them, tears have welled up in her eyes and spilled down her cheeks.

Jess has been accused of cheating in a recent exam and a disciplinary hearing is to be arranged, which could result in her failing her class or even being asked to leave the university altogether. Her whole future could be in ruins.

The afternoon light fades from the window, and still Jess sits there, numb with shock. She knows she has done nothing wrong, but she cannot imagine how she will prove this. Suddenly there is chatter and a giggle from the corridor outside, which she barely hears, then the door comes crashing open and Emily erupts into the room, her cheeks rosy and her face alight from her lunch date.

When she sees Jess sitting in the gloom she halts, wondering, then runs forward and crouches in front of her friend, putting her hands on her knees.

"Jess, Jess, what is it? Whatever has happened?"

It is some time before Jess can tell her, between sobs, what she has been told. Emily's face hardens as she listens.

"The effing bastards!" she snarls, "How dare they do this to you ... when you've worked so hard this term. Anyone who knows you knows you would no more cheat than cut your own head off!"

They sit and talk, never bothering to turn on the lights, while the winter evening draws down and the room becomes quite dark. As night-time draws on, Emily gets to her feet and goes to turn on the lights. Her friend's face, still tearstained but now filled with hope and happiness, follows her.

"So sod 'em," says Emily. "I'll see what my dad's solicitor thinks. Worst case scenario: if they throw you out, they can throw me out as well. I won't stand for this. Where you go, I go too. That's how it's always been with us."

## Ngetal ⧣ Healing, Cleansing, Renewal.

Corresponds to our sound ng, as in *sing*, or to the tilde-accented N sound used in Spanish, as in *mañana*.
**Pronounced NYED-ul or NYET-ul.**
**Tree:** Ngetal offers several choices. It may be the broom or the bracken fern: *Pteridium aquilinum;* the reed: *Phragmites australis;* or wheat-straw; and confusingly other plants are associated with it as well.
**Male/female (changeable)**
**Rune:** Nauthiz.
**Tarot:** The Four of Swords.
**Deity(ies):** Blodeuwedd, Dianecht, all Gods and Goddesses of healing.
**Correspondences:** Colours: pale green or blue. Crystals: aquamarine and jasper. **Planets:** The Sun, Venus, Pluto.
**Element:** Earth.
**Sabbat:** Imbolc.
**Living Things:** Kingfishers, geese, owls, broom, fern, reeds and rushes, guelder rose, water mint.

**Broom** is a common plant in the UK, a low-growing shrub that looks a little like gorse but minus the savage spines, and crowned in the summer with glorious egg-yolk yellow flowers. The brooms belong to three subdivisions of the leguminous *Faboideae* family, but the two best known are *Cytisusscoparius* and *Planta genista.* The latter gave one of our Royal families its name, Plantagenet, as sprigs of the plant were worn by followers of this dynasty, which gave us many kings from Henry II to Richard III. **Ferns** are one of the most easily recognised of all plants, loving wet and wild places. **Reeds** are not one family, but the name used for tall grass-like plants that grow in wet places, such as the banks of rivers, and this type of plant is found all over the world, wherever there is water. **Wheatstraw** is familiar to anyone who has dealings with livestock. Technically a waste product of cereal production, it has many uses in agriculture and the care of animals.

**Range: Broom:** Europe, North Africa and Asia. Many of these plants regenerate quickly after wildfires and love dry sandy soils, and it is so successful that it has been declared a pest in some countries. **Ferns:** This ancient primitive plant was around when the dinosaurs walked the Earth and is still very widespread. The many species of ferns grow in diverse habitats across the world, with most in moist tropical places and least in very cold places. **Reeds** grow worldwide, wherever there is water or wet ground. **Wheatstraw** can be taken to mean any straw left after a cereal crop has been threshed.

**Healing Properties:** Broom contains the diuretic scoparin and has been used to treat heart failure as it is beneficial in cases where patients are dropsical. It is also good for urinary tract infections such as cystitis, and the flowers have been used to treat gout. The huge diversity of ferns makes it impossible to provide a full list of their properties but they have been used for stomach aches, diarrhoea, worms and other intestinal problems. Reed has been used as a tea for digestive problems and placed on the skin to sooth insect bites. Some cereal straws have been used in healing, notably oat straw, which is rich in calcium and has a beneficial effect on the liver and pancreas, as well as on skin disorders such as eczema when applied externally. Straw can also be used for the health of a pond: thrown onto the surface, it has properties which will clear choking algae and leave the water clearer.

**Uses:** Broom was commonly used in the manufacture of ... brooms! Its short but sturdy and flexible branches are perfectly suited to this use and a bundle of broom twigs was probably used for tidying up in primitive homes long before man got around to fitting a wooden handle. Like the reed, it has been used for thatching roofs. Many varieties of decorative broom have been developed and are grown in parks and gardens for their colourful flowers and sweet scent. Bracken fern was once an important commodity to rural people, who had many uses for it, including bedding and even food for livestock, firing and fertiliser. Although many are toxic, some species of ferns can be eaten if cooked. They have long been valued as additions to gardens and as house plants. Reeds are still used today in thatching (Norfolk reed being the most popular type of roofing) and also for weaving of baskets and other items, as components in musical instruments and pens. It has also been used as fodder for animals. Straw has a wide range of uses and has even been used in construction, but its commonest use is for bedding for livestock and caged pets.

**Myth and Story:** The beautiful and faithless Blodeuwedd was made from flowers, including the broom, as a wife for Lew Llaw Gyffes, the unacknowledged son of the Goddess Arianrhod. In Irish mythology, broom was sacred to the God of Healing Dianecht (or Dian Cecht), who made a silver arm for King Nuada. When his own son Miach outdid him by creating a real flesh arm, Dianecht killed him out of jealousy. 365 healing herbs promptly appeared on the boy's body, each on the part of the body they would heal, and his sister Airmed began collecting them. But jealous Dianecht destroyed the herbs and the hope they brought. Fern seed was believed to make you invisible if you ate it, but the seeds themselves are hard to see, tiny and growing on the underside of the leaves. Paradoxically, the fern was also believed to restore the sight of a blind person. Greek mythology is full of stories of people being turned into plants as punishment or to protect them, and even reeds have their place: Zeus turned the nymph Syrinx into a reed to save her from the lustful depredations of Pan, who then cut the reeds and turned them into his musical pipes. In the Christian Biblical story, Moses was set adrift on the Nile in a crib made of reeds or rushes, echoing an earlier belief that the infant Horus was placed in a rush crib and protected from crocodiles by his divine mother Isis, and this is why crocodiles will leave a rush basket alone. Taliesin in Welsh legend was also set adrift in a reed basket by his mother, the Goddess Cerridwen. Reeds were an important resource for the ancient Egyptians, who used them extensively, even in the preparation of mummies, and they were the symbol of Upper Egypt (the southern half). Their whispering sound as they move in the breeze has caused them to be associated with the passing of secrets, as in the story of King Midas, whose barber was unable to live with the secret that his customer had donkey's ears, so whispered it to the reeds – who promptly whispered it to all and sundry! Straw has featured in many a magical story from traditional fairytales like *Rumpelstiltskin* and the *Three Little Pigs* to more modern stories like the *Wizard of Oz*. Cereals are also deeply symbolic of wealth, fertility and good fortune, but the part of the plant being considered is just the straw, which has also come to be associated with the renewal and cleansing of dirty conditions such as animals' pens and the prisons and lunatic asylums of the past.

**Magic:** Broom can be used in all cleansing rituals and rituals involving a "clean sweep". The plants associated with Ngetal have all been used for creating homes, whether in thatching, in construction or just as strewing herbs on a rough floor, and they all carry this meaning of protection of the family, of the home and of yourself and your lifestyle. Use them in spells of protection of you, your family, your personal space and your belongings.

**Divination:** This Ogham shares with Beith the sense of new beginnings, but in a very personal way, and with a sense of healing as well as renewal. This is about you: are you tired, stressed, unhappy? Go out and treat yourself to some really nice bath oil, some scented candles and maybe even a box of chocolates … It is time to take some space out for yourself, to nurture yourself and regenerate, start again. Look at your life and see where you need to make changes, sweeping away that which no longer serves you. Your need is for healing, for a chance to recoup, to gather your strength, for it may be needed. Do you dread going into work every day? Are you unhappy about your weight or how much you smoke? Are there deeper wounds in your life that need changes to be made so they can heal? Now is the time to take matters into your own hands and make those changes … for your own good.

**Reversed:** The *few* may speak of urgent necessity for change, and bad consequences if you ignore your own needs.

## Visualisation story

Nadine wears a headscarf and keeps her head lowered as she walks along the beach, not because it is cold, for it is a warm still evening. She has another black eye, and would rather not share this with any passer-by, who might ask *if she was all right,* as she does not have an acceptable answer to that question.

The Sun has gone down and the sea has turned a rich purple-grey, mirroring the sunset. Holidaymakers are leaving the sands now, returning to their hotels, chalets and apartments; rugs and picnic bags under their arms, children tired but still boisterous, sandy feet pushed into flip-flops and canvas shoes.

Slowly, slowly, the light leaves the beach and the Moon comes up. Nadine has walked the length of the sand, to the area beyond the rocks where people hardly ever bother to carry their deck chairs, rugs and food. The sea slops gently against the deserted beach, a movement too gentle to be called a wave.

It has been a long day and she is dog-tired. Nadine has two jobs because Tom is "between" jobs. When she gets in, there is a meal to prepare and housework to do. Tom is usually too busy "pursuing career opportunities" to do anything to help, as the litter of beer cans on the coffee table bears witness. The black eye is because she unthinkingly tutted yesterday, as she was gathering them up; she should really know better.

She feels dirty and sweaty and promises herself a long shower when she gets home. But the thought of going home at all fills her with dread. A wave of warm seawater slops over her foot. Nadine looks down and suddenly, without really knowing why, she is taking off her clothes. Cardigan, scarf, blouse, skirt, underwear, shoes all land in a pile on the rocks and she is wading into the water. It is delicious, warm and fresh simultaneously, easing her aching joints, soothing her bruises, cleansing her skin. Does she want to do a John Stonehouse? No, it is just a swim, so nice, and for once – something just for her.

Sometime later she climbs out of the sea and goes to her clothes, squeezing salt water from her hair. The pile of clothes is still where she left them, but a little white object has landed on the skirt, perhaps fallen from her pocket. She picks it up and by the bright light of the Moon she sees that it is the number of a women's refuge, something someone gave her months ago when she had been unable to hide or explain her bruises.

Nadine dresses, the card held in her teeth, her mind still and blank. She feels subtly different, healed, refreshed, stronger, as though the woman putting on the clothes is a different person from the tired, bruised, sad woman who entered the sea. Then she walks up the beach to Fore Street and enters a telephone box.

## Straif ⫲ Hurt, Conflict, Bad Change.

Corresponds to our letter Z or to Ts as in Tsar.

Pronounced STRAHF.

**Tree:** The blackthorn or sloe: *Prunus spinosa* and related spp.

**Male**

**Rune:** Thurisaz.

**Tarot:** The Tower.

**Qabalah:** Peh, the 27th path.

**Deity(ies):** The Cailleach, Hecate, the Morrigan, all triple- and crone Goddesses.

**Correspondences:** Colours: purple and black. Crystals: all black stones, agate, bloodstone.

**Planets:** Mars and Saturn.

**Element:** Fire and earth.

**Sabbat:** Imbolc and Samhuinn/Samhain.

**Living Things:** Black cats, black dogs, wolves, toads.

The **blackthorn** tree is most conspicuous in early spring, when it puts forth a sea of frothy snow-white blossoms, before its leaves have even started to shoot. Although it often grows right next to hawthorn (sometimes called whitethorn), to which it bears some similarities of form, it is not related, being a member of the cherry and plum family.

**Range:** The blackthorn is found across Europe and the Mediterranean region, Asia, North America and in parts of the African continent, as well as New Zealand. It is commonly found in hedgerows (where its vicious 10cm thorns make it a livestock-proof barrier) or in open woodland. When it grows alone in the open, it can achieve a height of around five metres.

Thorn trees across the world have been used for protection, of people, of towns and settlements, of land and of animals. At least one tree, Africa's "whistling thorn" *Vachellia drepanolobium* adds a further dimension to this by having its own "armed guards" living on its branches – aggressive ants which with unbelievable courage will attack any animal, even an elephant, which braves the tree's fearsome thorns and attempts to eat its leaves. Any tree of this fierce kind could be aligned to this Ogham *few*.

**Healing Properties:** Culpeper recommends using the berries for indigestion (despite their very acidic nature) and the leaves and powdered bark for diarrhoea and also as a laxative. He suggests using the berry juice as a gargle for sore throats and mouth ulcers, and for skin rashes; the tannins in the plant would render them effective for this, and they also contain a fair amount of vitamin C. The blossoms, gathered in spring and dried, are used for coughs, colds and breathing problems and there is some evidence that they act as a tonic on the kidneys and bladder.

**Uses:** The commonest use for this tree is as hedging, but the small blue-black fruits, or sloes, are famously used in the UK to make sloe gin, a traditional Christmas treat, and sloes are used for the making of similar products in other European countries. They can also be used for country wines, jam making, jellies and cordials, though they are extremely sour and need quantities of sugar added to render them palatable. Many winemakers believe in leaving them on the tree until the first frost has taken place, which makes them a little softer and milder in flavour. Our ancient ancestors may have eaten them as they were (without sugar!) as evidence has been found in excavated settlements of sloe pits, and evidence of sloes being used as food was found with the 5,300-year-old ice mummy Ötzi, found in the Ötzal Alps in 1991. The berries have also been used in the production of ink.

The tree is also used as a rootstock for domestic plum and cherry trees as it is a very hardy plant which grows in many different soil types. The timber is very hard and close-grained, and is used for small turned items such as handles and takes a very high polish. It has been used for walking sticks and famously for clubs like the Irish shillelagh, which was carved so that the bulky root formed the "business-end" of the club. It makes an excellent firewood.

**Myth and Story:** Though it hardly needs much protection but its own nasty thorns, the tree is closely guarded by a particular tribe of moon-worshipping Fae, who will punish anyone who damages it, especially during its own festivals of Imbolc and Samhain. In Christian mythology, this is another tree credited – if that is the right word – with comprising the crown of thorns worn by Christ.

**Magic:** As with the hawthorn, the nasty thorns (which are much longer than the hawthorn's) are excellent in protective witch bottles and have been used instead of pins by witches to pierce poppets when cursing someone. The tree and any item made from its wood, such as a wand or incense, is used primarily for cursing and banishing, as well as in protection spells and exorcism. An ancient spell calls for circling a fire three times before throwing a bunch of blackthorn twigs into it to summon the Wild Hunt! To dispel old unhappiness or guilt, push a blackthorn spine, one for each old hurt, into an apple while whispering an account of the original situation, then tie a thread to the fruit and hang it in the branches of the blackthorn tree to rot away.

**Divination:** Where the hawthorn speaks of emotional pain and humiliation, blackthorn goes a step further and indicates real harm, injuries, damage and serious strife – yes, that sounds like this Ogham *few*'s name, and it's a good way to remember its meaning. You will come up against someone or something that you will deeply regret encountering, and you need to be prepared if you are to overcome this. Your best way forward is with determination and courage, if you are to get past this serious obstacle. Other meanings of this *few* include a run of bad luck and changes for the worse, changes you do not welcome and which do not bring you ease or pleasure. This could be a health issue, or misfortune in your career or your private life. Yes, this all sounds quite negative, but this *few* has its positive gifts to offer as well, its meanings of protection and courage, of ability to deal with the misfortunes life throws in your path.

**Reversed:** Straif speaks of misfortunes and pain and its reversed appearance can only alter this subtly. It warns you to use extreme caution, as things may not go your way, and what is happening in your life is unpredictable. It is, however, a warning, not a threat, and Straif carries, as do all the Ogham *fews*, implied protection, just for its being there in your life.

## *Visualisation Story*

"I'm afraid it is what we thought," says the doctor, his eyes firmly fixed on his screen, perhaps because he needs to prepare himself a little before he can meet theirs.

Nan gives a little gasp of shock and grief. Phil clasps her hand in his and squeezes it tenderly, but he sets his jaw and keeps his eyes on Dr Banerjee, waiting for further information.

Finally, the doctor turns away from his computer and faces them, swivelling his chair and leaning forward a little, hands on his knees, the attitude of someone who cares and has advice to impart.

"It isn't very good news," he says quietly, "but we were rather expecting it, with your medical history, yes?"

Phil nods and beside him Nan stifles a sob and starts searching through her handbag for a handkerchief.

"There is a treatment ...." he says, hesitantly. Phil and Nan turn towards him at once, their faces changing. Nan lowers her handkerchief into her lap.

"It is a lengthy process and may be quite painful," says Dr Banerjee, the tone of his voice making it clear that "very painful" is what he really means. "Of course, there are many alternative therapies I could suggest instead...."

"But they won't work as well?" says Phil, responding to the doctor's unspoken words.

Dr Banerjee shakes his head. "They may give you a few more months, but that is all. But many people prefer that to the treatment I mentioned, which can take up to six months and may leave you with some residual ill effects."

Nan speaks for the first time. "Phil, whatever you want to do, it's your decision."

Phil looks at his wife of 40 years, remembering all they have shared and endured and achieved together. She is grey-haired now, with deep wrinkles around her eyes and mouth, but to him she is every bit as beautiful as she was at 24, and he has no desire to leave her yet.

Turning, he looks Dr Banerjee squarely in the eyes. "How soon can I start the treatment?" he says, and observes the doctor's look of pleased respect.

## *Ruis* 卌 *Judgement and Rehabilitation.*

Corresponds to our letter R.
Pronounced RWEESH.
**Tree:** The elder: *Sambucus nigra* and related spp.
**Female**
**Rune:** Isa.
**Tarot:** Judgement.

**Qabalah:** Samekh, the 25th path.

**Deity(ies):** Cardea, Hecate, Hel, Holda, Saturn, Venus, all crone Goddesses.

**Correspondences:** Colours: black, dark green and dark red. Crystals: olivine and jet. **Planet:** Venus.

**Element:** Water.

**Sabbat:** Samhuinn/Samhain.

**Living Things:** Pheasants, all black members of the crow family, black animals, dandelions.

One of the most magical of trees, **elder** is surrounded by a thick web of belief, stories and myths, from ancient tales of witches who could transform themselves into the tree to the elder wand in the *Harry Potter* stories. A smallish tree, it can be spotted from a long distance away when in flower, from late May into June, by the huge creamy flower heads, often as large as 25cms in diameter.

**Range:** Sambucus species are found across the Northern Hemisphere and subtropical regions of the Southern Hemisphere such as Asia, South America and Australasia, while *S. nigra*, the European elder familiar to people in Britain is also found across North America. It grows in any soil, but likes a lot of nitrogen, so grows readily in farmyards and other areas where animal waste might be found. A resilient and quick-growing tree, it will set itself in any patch of ground, from a gap in a country hedge to a corner of a fence or wall in a city centre. Common in hedgerows and open woodland, it has also found popularity as a garden and park specimen and variously coloured varieties, some with lacy leaves, have been developed. Elders and their close cousins are found pretty well across the world.

**Healing Properties:** As noted in Chapter Four, the various components of this tree have a wide range of healing properties and the fruits especially contain a range of micronutrients and vitamins, but it has also come under scrutiny by medical science recently as a possible answer to the symptoms of Covid-19. The plant contains sambucol, a powerful antiviral chemical, which could help patients afflicted with the virus, especially those who cannot receive the vaccination for some reason.

Elder also has uses on the dressing table. A tea made from the blossom is an excellent skin tonic and also benefits hair, particularly fair hair, bringing a golden sheen when used as a rinse. The elder will not often be attacked by pests due to its foetid smell and the leaves can be used to keep insects away, perhaps worn as a wreath on the head (when it will also cool you on a sunny day) or hung in the window to deter them from entering the house. Branches were hung in kitchens and dairies to keep away flies, or sprigs of leaves were hung around horses' necks for the same purpose. The leaves can also be stewed in water and the cooled brew used to drench plants to keep off pests, or elder leaves can be laid around plants you wish to protect from insect attack.

**Uses:** Elder has long been grown near human habitations for its beauty and its ability to keep away insects, while the berries, which though they are not especially pleasant to eat raw, being bitter and gritty, can be made into very nice jams, jellies, cordials and wines and have also been used in dyeing, notably in traditional Harris tweed. The attractive and fragrant blossoms can be made into elderflower cordials and "champagne" or dipped in batter and fried to be served with sugar. The tender shoots can be boiled or steamed like asparagus.

The tree is small and the timber therefore not adequate for building or other large-scale woodwork, although it can be turned into smaller items and the smaller twigs can be hollowed out to make panpipes.

**Myth and Story:** One of the most magical trees and beloved of witches, elder has always been at the centre of folk beliefs. "You burn your luck if you burn elder," said the country folk of old and to this day many people will not add it to a garden bonfire or their cottage woodpile. Cutting down the tree was sure to bring bad luck, starting with the appearance of the Elder Mother, a hag who would seek immediate vengeance for the loss of her tree. One belief told that if you stand under an elder tree at midnight on Midsummer's Eve, you will be able to see the Fairy King and his retinue riding by.

The tree is protective and should be grown near the house, and one old belief called for mothers to bury the shed milk teeth of their small children among the roots of the elder, which would then protect the little ones from harm. The tree was believed to protect dairy cows and keep them in milk, so was often grown near the byre.

Like the yew, elder has associations with death and the dead and is often found in churchyards. Wendy was told its relative scarcity in Cornwall was due to the very strong Methodist movement here cutting down the trees so their fruit could not be used by sinners to make wine!

Christians say it was the wood used to make Christ's cross, and that Judas Iscariot hanged himself from an elder tree after the crucifixion (unlikely, given the size of the tree!). Elder trees were once believed to house witches or be witches in disguise. In some beliefs elder would keep witches away, in others, witches would meet under the tree because it was so sacred to them. Witches love elder for all sorts of reasons, not least because it shows the three Goddess colours of white (the blossoms), red (the leaves turn red in late summer) and black (the berries). Despite having these colours, which represent all three faces of the Goddess in neopaganism, it is generally considered a crone tree, connected to crone Goddesses like Hecate. Its association with witches has led in Christian times to its being considered a tree of evil omen.

The legend of the Rollright Stones in Oxfordshire has Mother Shipton (a real person called Ursula Southill who actually hailed from Yorkshire) turning a king and his men into the stones and then becoming an elder tree herself.

**Magic:** A tree special to witches everywhere and connected with Hecate, the elder has many uses in magic. Although its wood is light and pithy, it can be used to make wands for psychic protection and other work, and a whistle made from the hollowed-out stem can be used in ritual to summon spirits. The twigs can also be hollowed out and cut into beads which, threaded on a string, can be used for wish magic or protection, as can the leaves. The elder is also used in banishing and exorcism, and workings to return evil magic to the sender. The tree is associated with the numbers five and thirteen – both especially magical to neopagans.

**Divination:** Elder speaks with the voice of the Goddess, bringing you spiritual insights, dreams and blessings. A lucky *few*, it speaks of wisdom and knowledge, perhaps gained at some cost and effort, but now there for you to use. But it is also connected to fate, to karma, to ineluctable destiny, and to personal obsessions and deep-rooted negative feelings, perhaps from the distant past, which need addressing, like shame, guilt, jealousy, anger and the need for revenge. It can mean judgement and even nemesis or it can indicate regeneration: it would be an interesting *few* to draw about a person serving a jail sentence, for example.

**Reversed:** The stave can speak of those negative thoughts in a very difficult way; you need to deal with them, not let them fester as you have been doing or things will get very much worse. This could also refer to another person, who may harbour these thoughts towards yourself. Either way, it speaks of a world of potential harm.

## Visualisation Story

A deeply unhappy man throws himself on the ground under an elder tree, overcome with guilt and desperation about something he did years ago which caused shame and misery, ultimately breaking up his family. For years he has kept this feeling inside him, gnawing away at his heart, unwilling to acknowledge it, even to himself, but striving always to bury it deep within him. No one else left alive now knows what he did; there is no one to whom he can make amends, apologise or explain. Recently the memories have been coming to the surface again, he does not know why, eating away at him, tormenting him with guilt and misery.

Today he came for a walk in the woods near his home, hoping to find a little calm space in which to escape from his feelings, and for a time the peace of the woods assuaged his guilt and he enjoyed a brief respite from it, focusing instead on the beauty of the autumn leaves, the birdsong, the slight and quite pleasurable chill in the air. But as he walks on, the feelings come over him again and he stops, with his hands over his face, still tormented.

By the path at the next bend an old elder tree grows, its twisted branches hung with glossy fruit in huge bunches, its leaves still vivid green against the autumn leaves with just a touch of red and yellow here and there. The tree seems to beckon him and he walks towards it, then throws himself down on the ground beneath. Something about the tree, perhaps its shade, perhaps its heavy scent, lulls him, and he relaxes a little, curls into a foetal position and lies, musing. Before long he has fallen deeply asleep.

He dreams. A tall old woman in a black cloak comes to him; her bright eyes search his face, seeing all he has hidden, knowing all his secrets, just as though he were made of glass. She nods once, then touches him on the shoulder, dismissing him, and turns away without anger or contempt.

He awakens. He stretches, gets up slowly, like an injured man trying to gauge how badly he is hurt, then stands, waiting. The burden he has carried for so long has fallen away; in its place is a new knowledge: I can do better. There is nothing I can do about the past, but I can work hard in the future to do better, to be better. Fleetingly, he sees the old woman's face in his mind and she smiles approval. He goes to the tree and takes a small elder twig from the ground beneath, wrapping it in his handkerchief to take away as a keepsake to remind him of this new beginning.

# AICME 4

The vowel sounds may be represented by full-size flescs running through the ridge horizontally, or by smaller dots placed through the ridge.

## *Ailm* ✦ *Joy, Love, New Beginnings.*

Corresponds to our letter A.
Pronounced AHLM.
**Tree:** The Scots pine: *Pinus sylvestris.*
**Male**
**Rune:** Daggaz.
**Tarot:** The Sun.
**Qabalah:** Resh, the 30th path.
**Deity(ies):** Attis and Cybele, Bacchus, Dionysus, Horus, Osiris, Poseidon.
**Correspondences:** Colours: piebald, of two or more colours. Crystals: parti-coloured stones such as agates.
**Planet:** Mars.
**Element:** Air.
**Sabbat:** Alban Arthan/Yule – it is associated with the day after the solstice.

**Living Things:** The lapwing, piebald creatures such as magpies, cows and horses.

The **Scots pine** will be familiar to everyone, though they may not know it by name. A tall and sturdy evergreen tree with a raw-boned appearance, it grows branches in straggly clumps, commonly with wispy remnants of died-back branches below them, leaving large sections of the trunk and major boughs bare. The long, tough needles are a very deep green and the cones are the classic pinecones children love to collect in the woods, child's fist-sized and conical with a flattish end.

**Range:** Scots pine is native to Northern Europe, where it will grow in quite wintry climates. Once native to the UK, it became a victim of global warming after the last Ice Age, and now occurs naturally only in Scotland but has declined there as well, thanks to deer grazing and felling for timber. But thanks to being an important crop in forestry, its soft, fast-growing wood being much in demand, it is still very common throughout the UK.

Conifers are the oldest trees on Earth, dating back to the Carboniferous Period, before the dinosaurs, when they helped lay down fossil fuels – the coal and oil we are still using today. Conifer means "bearing cones". The different varieties tolerate between them a wide range of habitats, from the Arctic Circle to the parts of the Sahara Desert which permit plant life to grow, so are found just about everywhere on earth.

**Healing Properties:** Astringent, aromatic and resiny, pine needles have been used to make cough and cold remedies, either as a tea or by inhaling the vapours from crushed needles placed in hot water. A Bach flower remedy from pine is said to restore feelings of self-worth. Pine is famously antiseptic and a tea made from the needles can be dabbed on injuries, burns or sores to ward off infection. The tea is also said to benefit arthritis and rheumatic joints.

**Uses:** Scots Pine is grown for its timber, which is used in a variety of ways, including the building and shipbuilding industries, for furniture, and also pulped for paper products. Its resiny timber does not decompose quickly which, with its tall, straight trunk, has led to its use as telegraph poles. It makes an excellent firewood and will burn well with no need for seasoning, though it may cause the chimney to become tarry over time. Before the petro-chemical industry, tar was produced from pines, and still is in some regions, also turpentine and rosin. Pine is associated in our minds with fresh air and cleanliness, so its fragrance has been used in toilet cleaners, bath essences, air fresheners and scented candles.

Scots pine is also used to manufacture a cloth called vegetable flannel which was invented in the nineteenth century and is used for hypo-allergenic clothing and blankets. In the US, the Scots pine is popularly used as a Christmas tree, whereas in the UK we prefer the silver fir (Robert Graves has the silver fir for Ailm in his tree calendar, but of course it was never a native of Britain). The Scots pine is also grown in parks and gardens, and cultivars have been developed with smaller, more compact shapes and with colourful foliage in blues and golds.

Pine nuts have become increasingly popular with the increase in vegetarianism but have long been used in foodstuffs such as pesto and baclava, baked into cakes and biscuits or toasted and sprinkled on salads and into casseroles. The nuts of Scots pine are a little too small to be used commercially but they are also edible. They are rich in vitamin E.

**Myth and Story:** The pine was associated with the legend of Cybele and Attis in Phrygian mythology. Her shepherd lover Attis proving unfaithful, Cybele drove him mad and he committed suicide by castrating himself, an action of self-mutilation subsequently emulated by the priests of his cult. The grieving Goddess then changed him into a pine tree which was ceremonially burned and he was reborn three days later. The Attic cult later spread to the Roman Empire, where a pine tree would be ceremonially cut down and brought to the temple, where it was worshipped as a God at the spring festival.

Another fertility God, Dionysus, is often depicted carrying a staff topped by a pinecone, as is the Norse God Freyr, the ancient Egyptian Osiris, and even the Pope today still carries a staff topped by a carved cone – symbolising enlightenment. Due to the practice of mummification, the ancient Egyptians were familiar with the internal organs of the body, and it perhaps did not escape their notice that the pineal gland (at the centre of the brain and associated with the third eye and spiritual awakenings) looks very much like a pinecone.

Perhaps because of its phallic shape, the pinecone was associated with fertility in many cultures, and today neopagans make phallic wands topped with a pinecone (or an acorn) to represent and invoke the God at the early spring Sabbats. A phallic wand of this kind is laid beside the Brideog (a doll created to represent the Goddess Bride) at Imbolc, to fertilise the Goddess for the coming year.

An old folk belief states that it is impossible to grow seven pines in a group: the seventh planted will inevitably die, so you must plant less or more than seven if they are to prosper.

**Magic:** Pine is useful in fertility magic and also cleanses and protects against negative influences, so that smudging with pine or burning pine as an incense will clear a room or a house of evil influences, just as effectively as sage. A wand of pine wood will encourage good energies. Pine, perhaps as an essential oil, can clear the mind and spirit of anxiety when used in an oil burner or even added to a hot bath.

**Divination:** "Strength through joy" – no, nothing to do with Nazi leisure activities – is a good way to think of this Ogham *few*. It is about joy in the sense that we tend to experience more when we are children; the kind of tingly, wonderful excitement we get on Christmas Eve, when the tree is decked with chocolate goodies and Santa is on his way with a sack full of presents for us. As adults we experience this more rarely, and for a spiritual person it tends often to be associated with their religious practice, and even with the state of being some have called "a state of grace." It can be associated with learning a new skill or finding a new lifestyle choice or even a new job, and this joy then feeds through into the spirit, bringing a strength and resilience that comes from the pleasure felt. Someone with a new car, for example, may feel invincible; how much more so someone who has found a new spiritual path and knows it is the right one for them? So Ailm is also associated with new beginnings, with changes and endings.

Ailm may also indicate love and the happiness and inner strength that comes not only from being in love, but from being in a firm, happy, stable relationship, or from a happy supportive family, knowing that you are loved and that all is well. It can mean the joy of a woman or a couple when they find they are pregnant, or the joy of having a newborn baby in your arms, having come through the pain of birth, the joy of watching older children playing in the garden or taking part in their school sports day. If you have experienced this kind of feeling, which comes somewhere between ecstasy and contentment, you will recognise that it brings a lot of strength with it, shoring up your mind, your spirit, even your body – happier people tend to be healthier.

**Reversed:** The *few* can speak of the opposite kind of feelings: fear, worry, anxiety and even downright panic, perhaps connected with loss.

## Visualisation Story

"You did really well!" Sam tells the boy. "Keep this up, and we'll be giving you your black belt in a few weeks."

Harry looks up at him, his small, freckled face filled with pride and happiness. He has worked hard since joining the school and Sam has watched him transform from a quiet, sad-eyed little boy into a much more dynamic, confident one. The classes seem to have filled him with happiness, joy in his new skills and in the friends he has found here. Sam is prepared to swear Harry has even grown a couple of inches taller, or maybe it is just that he now holds himself much straighter, looking people in the eye, where before he crept around the edges of rooms and corridors, trying to be invisible.

Sam thinks maybe it is good to mix a little serious advice with praise for most pupils and he does not want Harry to get overconfident. So, he ruffles the youngster's hair and says, "But you are going to have to work on that elbow strike – you aren't quite there with that yet." For a moment he almost regrets his words; he knows Harry has had a hard time with the other kids at the secondary school where he started last September and needs all the encouragement he can get, but Harry looks up and rewards him with a brilliant, toothy smile. "I will," he promises.

"Off you go now," Sam says, "don't forget your school bag."

Harry goes into the changing room and takes off his white *gi*, putting on his school uniform and his shoes. Then he shoulders his school bag and leaves the building, closing the door quietly behind him. He feels nine feet tall.

Further along the street he sees Jack and Ethan swinging off the railings by the public library. They see him coming, grin at one another and detach themselves from the ironwork. Harry remembers many previous occasions when they have followed him from school, sneering at his red hair, his slightly crooked teeth, his freckles and his small size; pushing him and tripping him when they got the chance. It all seems a long time ago now.

Reaching them, he puts down his school bag and smiles. It is not a friendly smile. Jack and Ethan pause in their approach.

"Hello," murmurs Harry quietly, still smiling. *I'll get that elbow strike right this time, I know I will,* he thinks.

Harry does not get the chance. The two larger boys have slid away from this confident, smiling little warrior and have vanished inside the library, Ethan muttering something about having left his bag behind. Time passes, but they do not come out.

## *Onn or Ohn* ✚ *Hope, Prosperity, Sex, Fertility.*

Corresponds to our letter O.
Pronounced UHN.
**Tree:** The furze, win or gorse: *Ulex europaeus.*
**Male**
**Runes:** Sowelu and Fehu.
**Tarot:** The Star.
**Qabalah:** Tzaddi, the 28th path.
**Deity(ies):** Jupiter, Lugh, Thor, all sun Gods.
**Correspondences:** Colours: yellow and gold. Crystals: amber and topaz.
**Planet:** Mars.
**Element:** Fire.
**Sabbat:** Ostara.
**Living Things:** Bees, hares, hawks, heather.

On moorland and hillside, on rocky slopes and rough land, **gorse** brings sunshine on the dullest day with its bright egg-yolk yellow blooms, which appear all year round. An old rhyme remarks, *"Kissing's out of fashion when gorse is out of bloom."* But as *Flower Fairies* creator Cicely Mary Barker went on to say, this never happens:

*"At every time of year,*
*You'll find one piece of blossom,*
*A kiss from someone dear."*

The rough beauty of this scrubby plant is a common sight in most wild places, with its dark green prickles, which are adapted leaves, and the gold flowers, which have a delicious fragrance somewhere between vanilla and almond.

**Range:** While the common gorse *Ulex europaeus* is native to Europe, there are many related species of thorny, scrubby plants that have spread across the world or have been deliberately introduced and have thrived because of their hardiness and resistance to conditions such as thin or poor soil, scarcity of water and salty sea winds. The delicate ecology of Australia is one habitat which has been threatened by this plant, which has also colonised much of the US. There is hardly a region of the world which does not have it in one form or another.

**Healing Properties:** Not many medicinal uses are recorded for gorse but historically it was used to treat jaundice (as its deep yellow flowers suggested this use under the Doctrine of Signatures) and kidney stones. Its younger shoots can be made into a diuretic tea and the Bach flower remedy based on gorse is for hope, for people who are very hopeless and depressed. The seeds are said to have been used as a repellent against fleas.

**Uses:** While the plant can be used as a rough hedge, its principal use has been for animal fodder as despite its thorns it is very nutritious and farmers might even chop or mill the plant to make it easier for livestock to eat. The pretty flowers are also edible for humans and can be incorporated into salads or candied and used to decorate cakes and puddings. The plant burns well and with much heat, even when green, and makes a good kindling and even a fuel in regions where more solid wood is harder to find. Although it does not develop a great deal of timber, the small pieces that do grow are used for handles, particularly for cutlery.

Being burned is part of the natural cycle of the plant and it was once fired deliberately in the late spring, so it would regenerate and produce fresh growth for fodder. As a habitat, it is vital for many birds, mammals, reptiles and insects, as well as the larger ungulates that feed off it.

**Myth and Story:** This plant was seen as deeply protective, especially from spiteful fairies which were repelled by its prickles. Branches of the gorse might be laid around the bed of a person suffering from sleeplessness or night terrors, to keep the sprites believed to be responsible from getting near the sufferer.

**Magic:** The brilliant yellow colour of the gorse blooms has caused it to be associated with the Sun, gold and with eggs (and thus fertility and wealth) and it is a component in rituals for the Sun and at Alban Eilir/Ostara, when eggs for a ritual might be dyed with the flowers, which give a rich yellow. Eggs are commonly used in magic and rituals of hope and new beginnings and the gorse might also be brought into the ritual space as branches and blossom to decorate the altar, as well as having the Ogham *few* on the altar and as part of any sigil created for the work. Use gorse for spells for wealth, especially the golden blossoms, which are always available.

The protective nature of the plant can be invoked by planting it close to the home and to the front border of the property, or even hanging small pieces of it inside the front door or windows.

**Divination:** Onn is gold coming into your life, perhaps at a time when you most need it. This may be a cash windfall of some kind, or a piece of good luck that improves your fortunes generally. The Celts associated the fragrance of the yellow blooms with sex and this is another meaning of this Ogham *few*: perhaps your fortunes are about to change in another way, with the object of your desires becoming inclined towards you. Its connection with fertility may also indicate a pregnancy, or it could be something as mundane as your vegetable garden delivering a huge crop of courgettes! Whatever form it takes, the key word for this *few* is hope, when you have been deprived and suffering for a long time. The Sun has come out, the gorse shines like gold and your life is about to get better. Gorse speaks of safety and security in the sense of financial wellbeing: of the confidence and contentment that comes with knowing you have enough – enough money, enough food, a roof over your head and no debts or worries.

**Reversed:** Onn speaks of the loss of hope, of the wreck of your plans and financial loss, or of a disappointment in love.

## *Visualisation Story*

Anil comes in through the back door, as he usually does, calling, "Mamaji!" His mother is old-fashioned and likes to be addressed like this instead of the more usual "mum". It is Mother's Day and he has flowers for her and a pretty card he found at the newsagents.

"Mamaji?" he calls again, and his mother appears in the kitchen doorway, her lined face smiling under her greying hair. To Anil she is and always will be beautiful. "Where's dad?" he asks.

"In the potting shed, as usual. I don't know what he does in there all day … smoking, I expect, and you know what the doctor said about that …"

Anil stops his mother's homily by the simple expedient of kissing her, then hands her the card and flowers. "Happy Mother's Day," he says, smiling. The aroma of sweet Indian pastries in the kitchen has not escaped him: is that balushahi he can smell? Is it a special occasion? He cannot imagine his mother would have made them for herself, Mother's Day or not.

Then there is the pleasure of seeing his mother open her card and of hearing her exclaim over the flowers, of the hunt for a suitable vase and the cutting of the cellophane and the sharp aroma of the flower stalks.

"Roses," she says, putting them to her nose, even though florists' flowers never have any scent. "How beautiful. What a good son you are."

The back door opens and his father appears, a newspaper under his arm and a mint in his mouth: if he has been smoking in the shed, there's no need to let Mamaji know about it.

"Anil!" he cries, hugging his son. He admires the flowers and card, then goes through to the lounge. "Bring us some coffee, Lathi," he says, "and some of the balushahi, please. I know it's his favourite."

A little later the family are licking their fingers happily, pleased to be together with good coffee and sweets to eat. Then Anil's father clears his throat.

"How is the business?" he asks, lapsing into Hindi to demonstrate his concern.

Anil sighs. "Could be better," he mutters. "Trust something like Covid to happen, just as I was getting started. It wasn't good luck. Things are a little better now, but ..." What he wants to say is that he needs a cash injection to get the business off the ground again, but he is conscious that his parents have already helped him, digging into their slender resources perhaps more than they could afford.

To his surprise, his mother is smiling and his father looks pleased as well.

"What?" he asks, bewildered.

His mother rises and goes to the mantelpiece, taking down an envelope from behind the clock. The Indian stamp on it catches his eye at once. She sits down and takes the letter out, smoothing it on her knee as though she is stroking a cat. Anil sits up, alert.

It is unexpected and wonderful news. His cousins in Jaipur have agreed to his marriage to their daughter, the clever, beautiful Geetika, who has just gained an Honours degree in business management. Anil has admired Geetika from afar for many years, has loved her without hope, judged all women by her standard. What she will bring to his business, including her dowry, is one thing; what she will bring to him as a man is like a dream come true.

## Ur or Uhr ✦✦✦ True Love, Marriage, Family, Ancestors.

Corresponds to our letter U.
Pronounced OO-r.
**Tree:** The heather: *Calluna vulgaris*.
**Female**
**Rune:** Ingwaz and Othila.
**Tarot:** The Lovers.
**Qabalah:** Zayin, the 17th path.
**Deity(ies):** Bride, Vesta, Hera and Juno, Isis, all deities of the household and family.
**Correspondences:** Colours: purple, white and amber. Crystals: pearl and amber. **Planet:** The Moon.
**Element:** Earth.
**Sabbat:** Litha.
**Living Things:** Bees, grouse, larks, mistletoe.

*All along the purple **heather,** will ye go, lassie go* …. This colourful plant always brings the Scottish Highlands to our minds, yet it is a common sight on moorland all over the UK and is grown in garden borders and tubs for its long-lasting purple (sometimes white) blooms and its sweetness for bees.

**Range:** If there is acid soil – heather will thrive. It grows across Europe and Asia Minor, building its own ecosystem and transforming (with other plants and mosses) into peat as it goes. It is a member of the large Ericaceae family, which grows pretty well everywhere across the world, in one form or another.

**Healing Properties:** Heather has a tonic effect on the urinary system, the kidneys and bladder, and can be used in the treatment of urinary tract infections like cystitis. Heather infusions can also be used to cure a cough and is an old folk remedy for aching joints. The honey derived from this plant may also carry some of this healing ability and can also be used on sores and skin rashes.

**Uses:** Heather has historically been used in remote regions for the thatching of homes, for making brooms and besoms, for fodder for livestock and as a fuel for cooking and heating the home. It would once have formed the matrix of crofters' beds. The cutting of peat has gone on for centuries, as the peat burns when dried, but also for the commercial production of potting composts, though efforts are now being made to find other sources for this product, in order to help conserve vanishing peat bogs and their associated habitats. Heather flowers give a glorious, rich, dark honey and have also been used to make ale, and a strong green or yellow dye can be made from the plant. Because heather is considered lucky, and white heather especially so, the plant has been made into keepsakes to sell to tourists in moorland areas.

**Myth and Story:** An iconic part of the Scottish landscape and well embedded in poetry and story, heather is also a national plant of Norway. It is connected with the Fae, and there are various stories of people who slept in the heather being taken by the Little Folk, or of people who were taken finding themselves lying in the heather the next morning. The rarer white heather is considered lucky because it is said to grow only upon ground where no blood has ever been spilled, while the purple heather's hue may be due to the blood spilled in battle.

**Magic:** It can be used magically to remove negativity, and as a smudge to cleanse a room or a home. Use the Ur symbol to help with grief or stress over the passing away of a family member, or over family problems generally.

**Divination:** Heather is the home, the fire and the bed within, where the married couple lie together and beget their children. In this same bed they will love, sleep, rest, nurse babies, endure sickness and finally die. So the heather speaks of family, of generations of children and parents and grandparents, of the inheritance of features and names and property, of legacies. It speaks of the partnership that is marriage, rather than of love and passion, as Onn the gorse does. It speaks of family and the many happinesses and tragedies that embody family, of happy events and of grief, of family secrets and people and things from long ago.

The regenerative powers of heather (which soon re-grows after burning) and the plant's use in the making of brooms also bring the meanings of cleansing, healing and new beginnings into this Ogham *few*.

**Reversed:** The *few* may speak of a threat to the relationship, perhaps even a marriage break-up and divorce. It could be something negative emerging from your family past which has the potential to cause you pain.

## *Visualisation Story*

"Oh no, not that one!" says Antonia worriedly. "It doesn't go with your dress anyway."

Sometimes Penny feels it is her mother's wedding, not her own, but she knows how much it means to her and that it is her mother's way of expressing her love, so she just agrees. The veil – Antonia is set on everything being as traditional as possible – was not Penny's favourite of the four they are looking at. Penny sighs a little; sometimes she thinks she and Con should run off, elope, and avoid the need for all this obsessing and spending. Or just live together as they are at present. But then, Penny wants a family, and Antonia has some strong and oft-expressed views on children turning up as bridesmaids at their own parents' weddings.

The weekend wears on, with visits to the dressmaker, the caterer, the printer, the baker, the candlestick-maker … or that is what it is beginning to feel like to Penny. She is almost looking forward to getting back to work on Monday. Arriving back at her parents' home, she gets out of the car a little wearily to find an old Mercedes sitting in the drive.

"Oh, who's this?" says Antonia, looking for her front door key in her jumbo handbag.

Malcolm greets them in the hall, a coffeepot in his hands. "Your aunt is here," he tells his wife, "Ethel, is it?" he adds vaguely.

In the drawing room a very old lady in a pale lilac twinset is seated by the fire, her thin legs outstretched towards it, although it is not a cold day. As they enter, she looks up and smiles a beautiful smile.

"Antonia! And … Phoebe?" she says.

"Penelope," says Antonia automatically and a little tactlessly. "Penny, this is your Great Aunt Edith, on my side, your grandmother's sister."

Malcolm brings in the coffee and some shortbread – Antonia always has good shortbread in case of callers – and they sit in silence for a while, savouring the refreshments. Then Edith lays aside her cup and speaks.

"I've brought you a present, my dear," she says. "You don't have to accept it if you don't wish to, but it has been in my family a very long time. I wore it, and so did your Grandmother, God rest her." She reaches down to a cloth bag at her feet and takes out a carefully wrapped parcel, which she hands to Penny. "Open it," she encourages.

Penny carefully loosens the string on the paper and opens it. A waterfall of snowy lace spills out onto her lap, handmade antique Venetian, absolutely priceless. She sits hardly daring to breathe, gazing at its unearthly beauty.

"H-how did you keep it so white?" she asks at last.

Edith shakes her head. "It's in acid-free paper, and before that we used to put it out when there was a frost. These old materials all have their secret methods." She reaches into her bag again and pulls out another parcel, which she opens herself. It is a large leather-bound photo album. "I thought you might like to see a few of the brides in the family who wore it," she says.

Penny takes the heavy book into her lap reverently, while Antonia picks up the costly veil and folds it with care, stowing it away in its specialist wrapper once more. The album opens at the first page: withered grey-brown images of a bride and groom long gone, carefully posed against a photographer's backcloth. The bride in a dull white gown of a former age and the groom in a uniform … WWI? The veil alone seems to stand out, drifting in a cloud of floral white down the woman's back, a fold of it coyly blown against the legs of her new husband.

"That's your Great Great Grandmother Lily," said Edith, "Sidney was given the Military Cross at the end of the war."

"It's too long," comments Antonia, wrinkling her brow. She had not worn it herself for this very reason.

"Of course, it can be altered," says Edith kindly.

Penny turns another page, and another. The faces of family stare back at her, strangers, yet not, sharers of her DNA. "No," she says firmly. "I don't care about fashion; I want to wear it just as it is." *And to be part of this*, her mind adds, *part of this wealth of heritage which I never knew I had.*

## Edad or Eadha ✦ Wealth, Prosperity, Overcoming Fear.

Corresponds to our letter E.

Pronounced EH-dad or EH-yah.

**Tree:** The white poplar: *Populus alba*or; the aspen: *Populus tremula*.

**Female (poplar), Male (aspen).**

**Rune:** Uruz andOthila.

**Tarot:** All the Kings, but especially the King of Pentacles.

**Deity(ies):** Cronos, Diana, Hecate, Hercules, Jupiter, Persephone, all crone Goddesses.

**Correspondences:** Colour: speckled red. Crystal: pearl.

**Planets:** Poplar: Saturn. Aspen: Mercury.

**Element:** Poplar: water. Aspen: air.

**Sabbat:** Alban Elfed/Mabon.

**Living Things:** Swans and other white animals and birds.

One of the most distinctive trees of the British countryside, the **white poplar** is well-named. Its trunk is white, like the silver birch, and it also sports pale green leaves with a silvery cottony underside which catches the light as they flutter in the breeze. The poplar and aspen family are all known for having a "trembling" habit, which is most noticeable in the aspen: the long flat leaf stalks and leaves dance in the tiniest breath of wind. The tree also rejoices in amazingly decorative bark, which would put many mosaic-tiled floors to shame. Its snowy white bark is patterned all over with dark diamond-shaped crevices, called lenticels, which are strikingly attractive. The poplar stands tall – literally. It has a typically fastigiate habit, which makes it look a little like a person standing with their arms raised above their head. The **aspen** is another tall tree, achieving 40 metres in height, and it shares the poplar's beautiful diamond-patterned bark, though it is pale grey-green rather than white.

**Range:** The white poplar tree grows across Europe, the Mediterranean, North Africa and Asia, and has now moved into Australia, where its success has caused it to be classified as a pest. There are many poplar species and, just to confuse matters even more, many of these have interbred. In the UK we have the white poplar, the black poplar and the Lombardy poplar (a Himalayan import which has the most noticeably fastigiate habit of the family), but also the aspen, a related species which is found in cool temperate regions of Europe and Asia, growing as far north as Iceland, and also associated with the Forfeda letter Eabadh. Hybrids of white poplar and aspen are called grey poplar.

**Healing Properties:** Poplar sap contains salicin, the root of aspirin, and this makes the plant useful in the treatment of aching joints and fevers. The trembling habit of the tree was recognised as a sign of its medicinal properties in the Doctrine of Signatures, and it was used for agues and fevers where the patient was shaking or trembling. Its healing qualities are very similar to those of quinine. The Bach flower remedy made from aspen is recommended for people suffering from fear and anxiety. A tisane made from poplar bark is a remedy for tiredness and poor appetite, and the buds can be infused in heated grease, such as coconut oil, and used externally for their antibacterial and anti-inflammatory qualities. The bark and young leaves can be boiled in water to produce an antiseptic wash which can also be taken internally as a general tonic.

**Uses:** Although very attractive, poplars are not usually grown in gardens, owing to their very strong and invasive root systems, which can seriously damage pipe-work and even foundations. It has been used as an ornamental tree in parks and open spaces, and also (because of its tolerance for salt) to reinforce coastal areas such as dunes. The soft wood of both the poplar and the aspen is used in the paper industry as well as the manufacture of packing cases and is roasted to make charcoal. Poplar wood is also used for sculpture.

**Myth and Story:** The poplar is yet another tree supposed to have been used to make Christ's cross, and it is supposed to whisper secrets if you stand beneath it. It was thus seen as an unlucky tree, and some would not plant it close to a home for this reason, though in other beliefs it was seen as lucky and protective. The tree was especially connected to the hero God Hercules, who wore it as a wreath when he entered Hades to drag out the fearsome three-headed dog Cerberus as one of his Twelve Labours. The sisters of Phaeton, the boy who came to grief when he drove the Sun's chariot, were turned into poplars because they mourned him so deeply. The white poplar was also sacred to Pluto, who created the tree from the body of his beloved Leuke, a nymph who lived out her life in his kingdom after he abducted her.

**Magic:** The tree's trembling habit has connected it with the idea of fear and courage and its leaves, bark and twigs are all used in magic to increase courage and diminish fears and worries. A sliver of the poplar's white, diamond-patterned bark is an excellent amulet for this purpose. An incense made from the bark and leaves can be used on the altar for magic of this kind, and a piece of the bark or a twig can be carried to increase wealth.

The protection of poplar and aspen is against thieves and financial loss, and the trees were once planted close to homes to ward off those who might break in and steal – to the detriment of the building's stability, one imagines.

**Divination:** Some diviners say they can judge when heavy rain is expected by standing under the tree and listening to the sounds the leaves make.

The poplar or aspen's pale leaves and trembling speak of fear, and fear is one of the meanings of the Ogham *few* Edad, but fear with its own reasons. Edad speaks of the ability to overcome fear, of the testing quality of fear and the opportunity to overcome it and thus prove oneself worthy, courageous, successful. *Screw your courage to the sticking point*, says this letter, for only so can you escape from the fear that has held you back, caused you to be less than your potential. Go on: do it, take a chance, and throw your fear to the winds that shake the aspen leaves!

The other meaning of this *few* is property and riches, and it is used magically to increase wealth. Sometimes the two are linked: many people know what it is to be in want, and to fear because they do not have enough money to feed their families or are perhaps in danger of losing their homes.

**Reversed**: Edad means being overcome, overwhelmed by your fears, so that you fail in your quest, fail at your career, fail in whatever you have set out to do. The reversed *few* can also speak of wealth in a negative way, of losing out, of poverty or of the less desirable things that come with wealth, like selfishness and greed.

## Visualisation Story

Jane hovers at the front door, then changes her mind, takes off her coat and goes back into the lounge, where she sits down with her head in her hands. Since her husband died she has become more and more terrified of leaving the house, so that her chest hurts and her knees shake when she approaches the front door. For over a year now, she has relied on her daughter or a kind neighbour to bring in groceries or post letters for her, and the gardens – once Bill's pride and joy – are now in a sad state of neglect, especially the front. Sometimes she can summon the courage to go and weed and tidy the back garden, but even this is getting rarer.

She thinks she will make a cup of tea to restore her nerves, so she gets up and is halfway to the kitchen when there is a knock at the door. It isn't Rachel's day for bringing shopping; she works on Wednesdays, so Jane wonders who it can be. She opens the door a crack. To her relief it is only Margaret, her kind neighbour. She opens the door wider.

Margaret breezes in, taking off her jacket and bringing in a fragrance of the day, the sharp scent of woodsmoke from someone's bonfire and the bitter tang of autumn leaves. She puts her bag down in the hall, but removes a paper bag.

"I brought us some pastries," she says, a little guiltily.

"Oh, how lovely, I'll put the kettle on," says Jane, smiling.

Some time later, as they sit licking sugar from their fingers, Margaret broaches the subject which has been on her mind.

"Jane, what are we going to do about you? You really can't spend the rest of your life shut in here alone, can you?"

Jane bows her head; she knows it is true, but does not know how to break out from her fear. Bill died of a heart attack just outside their gate and she cannot walk past that spot without reliving that awful moment all over again.

"I've brought you something," says Margaret. "Hayley made it for me ... you know she's into ...."

"Some strange things," says Jane rather primly. Once she was a regular churchgoer but the vicar, after one or two visits soon after Bill's death, has obviously given her up as a hopeless cause.

Margaret shrugs good-naturedly and takes a small gauze bag out of her pocket. "It can't hurt but might help," she recites in a humorous sing-song. In the bag are a few crystals, a slip of folded paper and a piece of wood with a strange symbol carved on it. "This is Ee-dad. I can't remember how you are really supposed to pronounce it, but it helps with fear and gives you courage. And there's a little bit about it, what it means and how to use it. It's Ogg-ham; that's an ancient magical alphabet like runes."

Jane accepts the bag politely and takes the Ogham *few* into her hand. Strangely, through all her scepticism, all her Christian belief that magic is nonsense, she feels a tingle of power in the thing. She weighs it in her hand and is silent.

"What do I do with it?" she asks eventually.

"Hayley wrote a little paper thingy and put it in there; it tells you what to do."

Jane begins to cry. Margaret is horrified and rushes over to comfort her. "I'm so sorry; I'm so sorry …. I never meant …. If it's too difficult …"

"No," says Jane, drying her eyes quickly. "That isn't it at all. It's just that … you've never given up on me, you and Hayley. I've been so silly. Maybe this is all it will take." She takes a deep, deep breath. "I want to try now."

Twenty minutes later they have been to the top of the street, turned the corner into the High Street, and come back again. Jane's eyes are bright and she holds the Ogham *few* tightly in her hand. It is still giving her strength and she knows that in the days to come she will walk out again, further and without Margaret, more and more often, until she has reconquered her old life.

## *Idad or Iodhadh* ✦✦✦✦ *Death or Endings, Reincarnation.*

Corresponds to our letter I.
Pronounced EE-da or EE-yoh.
**Tree:** The English or European yew: *Taxus baccata.*
**Male**
**Rune:** Eiwaz.
**Tarot:** Death.
**Qabalah:** Nun, the 24th path.
**Deity(ies):** Anubis, Arawn, Astarte, Artemis/Diana, Hades, Hecate, Hel, Osiris, Neith, Persephone, all Underworld deities.

**Correspondences:** Colours: black and dark green. Crystal: olivine.
**Planets:** Saturn and Pluto.
**Element:** Earth and water.
**Sabbat:** Alban Arthan/Yule.

The darkly crowned **yew** is a familiar sight in parks, gardens and particularly in churchyards, where huge and ancient specimens may be older than the church building itself. On female trees, its dark needles are set off by tiny cherry-red berries in autumn, which persist well into the winter. Very ancient trees may split and even fall over, but they continue to grow and send up new boughs, which has given the tree an association with rebirth and new beginnings, as well as death and mourning.

**Range:** The yew is found all across Europe and into Scandinavia (although the European yew does not do well in very cold regions) and also through the Middle East and down as far as North Africa. Other trees in the yew family are found across most of the world, including the Americas and Asia. It is one species that is predicted to prosper and increase its range due to global warming.

**Healing Properties:** This tree is extremely poisonous ... with the sole exception of the red, fleshy part of the berries – not the seed itself – which is eaten by birds. The plant contains many toxins, but the main one is taxine – a poison which attacks the heart. The yew's association with churchyards stems partly from the church's policy of planting yew trees in graveyards to prevent disrespectful farmers from grazing their cattle in them, as the cattle would eat the yew and die. The planting of yews may also have been instigated by the Christian policy of taking over pagan customs and converting them to Christianity along with the pagans themselves, so the yew, sacred to many pagans, would have been an obvious choice for associating with new Christian churches. The tree is also hyper allergenic. Some chemicals found in the yew, however, have been used in cancer treatments.

**Uses:** While the yew was used extensively in the past for all kinds of items, its relative scarcity now means it is not so commonly used, although small items such as cabinet handles and marquetry are still made from yew. The timber is unsuitable for construction work. Historically valued for the manufacture of weapons, the yew played a large part in warfare as it was used for the English longbow – the cutting-edge weapon of its time. It is now largely used only in gardens and as part of hedgerows. It is particularly suited to topiary and very old topiarised specimens may be seen in formal gardens everywhere.

**Myth and Story:** One of Britain's most ancient yew trees, the Fortingall Yew in Perthshire, estimated to be up to 2,000 years old, is said to mark the birthplace of Pontius Pilate, the Roman governor of Judaea who tried Christ. Some people have suggested that the tree, which is now protected within a walled enclosure, is closer to 9,000 years old. A portion of the tree, which is male overall, recently changed gender and bore red berries!

Shakespeare knew his plants and trees, as he demonstrated throughout his works, and "slips of yew, silver'd in the Moon's eclipse" form part of the witches' brew in *Macbeth*.

**Magic:** Strongly connected with the dead, yew is used in magic to summon the ancestors and raise the spirits of the dead. But its meaning of rebirth, regeneration and new beginnings can also be tapped into, and the wood can be burned as incense or as a smudge. It can also be made into dowsing rods, which work almost as well as hazel.

**Divination:** Yew is the tree of immortality as well as death, and its place as the last Ogham *few* of the set is appropriate, for it also speaks of new beginnings, of the cycle beginning again, just as a storm-felled yew will send up new trunks and start all over again. This *few* tells of encouragement, of the protection that the yew gives against evil, and of your own ability to overcome, to surf endings and move on to new things, new relationships, a new job, new ways of thinking. The *few* tells you something may be coming to an end but, as with the Tarot Death card, it will not necessarily mean you! Something has outlived its purpose in your life, something is leaving you, something is ending, as all things must. There may be grief involved, for this is a final ending, not a temporary farewell, but you must face this and let go. It may not mean the death of a person, for there are other things that die: relationships, beliefs, love, businesses, friendships, groups. The *few* implies that you may have to be the one to make the ending, to end the relationship, to get rid of the outworn item or situation. It could even be as simple as clearing out your wardrobe and chucking out those size 12 dresses you know in your heart you will never fit into again! It's for the best.

**Reversed:** It may speak of the bad things that could happen if you don't make these endings yourself, of the inadvisability of hanging onto the old at any cost.

## Visualisation Story

"And I don't wanna see you back here again, son," says Hutchings, opening the outer door. It is something he says to all the younger ones as they leave, though he knows he will see a good proportion of them back again.

Will does not reply, but picks up his bag, nods to the warder and goes out into the street. As he has expected, there is no one there to meet him. That life is over.

A watery sun shines down on him, but to Will it has all the beauty of a burning Mediterranean noon; he stands for some moments looking up at the sky, noticing the colour of the trees that line the road; how had he not known it was spring? Then he takes a piece of paper from his pocket and reads it. He picks up his bag again, wincing at its weight – he seems to have lost a good deal of muscle mass and fitness inside – and heads for the bus station, following the directions on the paper.

Two hours later he arrives at a shabby looking house in an anonymous street and knocks at the scratched dark blue door. After a moment it is opened by a short man in jeans and T-shirt, who greets him without looking him in the eye. Another ex-con; Will recognises the demeanour.

"I'm Peters," he says.

Wordlessly, the other opens the door wider, then disappears inside. Will shoulders his bag again and enters a small hall with a noticeboard on one wall covered in ageing posters and green post-its. As he stands there, a door opens opposite and a woman emerges. On seeing him, her face assumes a welcoming smile.

"I'm Sarah the manager," she says. "Did you find us without too much trouble? Let me show you around."

She takes him upstairs and shows him his room, then the fairly clean bathroom on the same floor, then leads him downstairs again to the kitchen, also fairly clean, and another room with a single bookcase and a further novelty.

"We have a computer!" she says proudly, directing his attention to a thick screened monitor. Will sees it is very outdated compared to the ones in prison, and nods. "When are you seeing your PO?" Sarah asks.

"Monday," says Will briefly.

Upstairs again he drops his bag on the bed, too tired and dispirited to unpack, other than removing a single item from the front pocket and laying it on the bedside cabinet. A crumpled photo of Megan. Stupid; that life is over, as he tells himself again. One visit, and after that not so much as a letter in 18 months. His own fault, he reminds himself, and what did he expect? Yellow ribbons on every tree?

Sarah puts her head around the door. "Someone to see you."

In the hall Megan is standing, wearing a coat he has not seen before. He manages to speak.

"How did you find me?"

"That don't matter now. I meant to be outside when … when you come out, but I missed the bus. But I'm here now. I've had a lot of time to think, and this is what I come to say. That it's all right, we ain't over. But you promise me this won't happen again, or we will be. Start over?"

Will too has had a lot of time to think and does not need to hesitate before making his promise – to her and to himself.

# 8

# The Forfeda

The Forfeda, which simply means "more letters", are five or more Ogham created at a later date to represent diphthongs and other sounds. They look quite different from the main Ogham and are a lot more complicated to reproduce on divination sets and wands. Unlike the original letters, some of them can be written with curved strokes. They were added bit by bit, much later than the development of the first five aicmes, when other races began to arrive in Ireland and the writing system needed to be able to represent sounds not found in Irish. They were in use in the mediaeval period but are not found in stone inscriptions.

The Forfeda struck us as a little like the human appendix when it came to divination: they probably had their uses once but are irrelevant now. But is this the case? Some Ogham practitioners use them and some appear to ignore them, and in the *Auraicept na n-Éces* they are included in some lists but not in others. Another problem with them is that no one seems to agree on the complete list; most sources include five or six symbols; others have up to thirteen (some lists include the V-shaped forms that start or finish the ridges, and even blank spaces between words). As the extra Forfeda are very obscure, on Sandie's advice we decided to concentrate on the six generally accepted ones, though even for these there is very little information available, so we have had to use our own magical knowledge and intuition to fill in a few gaps.

One suggestion for using the Forfeda is as confirmation or clarification of the Ogham *fews* already drawn from the main set, drawing one from the secondary letters when you need just that little bit more context. Because of the quite broad area to which these later *fews* seem to connect, they could be used for mapping, telling of which part of your life your casting speaks, for example, your health, your material wealth, your spiritual life. Cast them with the other *fews*, or afterwards on top of the main casting, and note to which groupings they lie adjacent. Iphin, for example, might mean your health, and Oir your money and property or your career.

We feel the Forfeda are like the later rune alphabets, the Futhorc and the Younger Futhark: you should take your own decision on their importance to your use of the system, but you should probably know your way around them "just in case".

Robert Graves had an intriguing approach to the Forfeda in his now almost unobtainable book, *The Crane Bag and Other Disputed Subjects* (1969), tying the Forfeda to the magical objects contained in the bag belonging to the Celtic sea God Manannan. In some Celtic legends Manannan had as a wife the beautiful Aoife, who was transformed into a crane by an enemy and spent the rest of her life in bird form. When she died, he made her skin into a bag to contain his most precious magical belongings, an eerie bag which seemed empty at low tide, and only at high tide (when Manannan's powers were at their height) could its contents be seen.

Many modern Druids carry a "crane bag" – the item was originally made from the skin of this bird – containing their sacred objects, their magical tools and talismans. The crane bag of Manannan contained a pair of shears, a helmet, the shoulder strap and hook of a smith, bones, his shirt, as well as other items such as a knife and a huge piece of a whale's back or backbone.

Note: by the time these extra letters were in use, the Ogham was used horizontally rather than vertically, perhaps because it was now exclusively used on paper media.

## Eabadh ᚛ Wisdom and Inspiration, Communion with the Dead, Achievement.

This is the diphthong EA, but can also represent the sound CH or K.

Pronounced: EH-vah or EH-bah.

**Tree:** The aspen, but this *few* is also sometimes called "the Grove".

**Female**

**Rune:** Jera and Laguz.

**Tarot:** The High Priestess and the Moon.

**Deity(ies):** Anubis, Arawn, Hades, Persephone, all Underworld deities.

**Correspondences:** Colours associated with this *few* are every shade of green, grey and silver. Crystal: black opal.

**Planet:** Mercury.

**Element:** Air.

**Sabbat:** Alban Elfed/Mabon and Samhuinn/Samhain.

**Living Things:** White flowers and animals, doves and swans.


The **aspen** is easily identified by its very mobile silvery foliage, which catches the eye as it flutters in the slightest breeze. Although the rounded triangular leaves are deep green on the top, the underside is a silvery white and is flashed as the leaves twist and turn in the air, even on a relatively still day when no other leaves are moving. This effect can be a little spooky, which is why this tree has been associated with the spirits of the dead and the Underworld.


**Range:** Aspens are found in cooler regions of the world, where cold winters and cool summers are usual. They are resistant to high winds, as their leaves are formed so as not to cause drag on the main branch; hence their wild fluttering in any breeze. They are another tree associated with regeneration as they can survive forest fires due to their very deeply plunging roots. The tree may be destroyed, but the roots soon send up suckers to create fresh growth. This habit has caused the tree to achieve great ages, not singly, but as colonies of regenerated trees.

Aspen species are found across the world, from the Arctic Circle to Africa, in the Americas as far south as Mexico, and an unrelated species called the white aspen, *Acronychia oblongifolia*, is indigenous to Australia.

**Healing Properties:** The aspen shares with several other trees the chemical salicin, the basis of our modern aspirin tablet. It is also anti-inflammatory and antibacterial, so is a useful tree for healing. It has been used for urinary tract infections, rheumatism and fevers, and externally for skin complaints like eczema and for frostbite injuries. Under the Doctrine of Signatures, the aspen was used for people with uncontrollable shaking, such as MS or Parkinson's. The Bach flower remedy aspen is for soothing needless fears and anxiety.

**Uses:** The soft white wood of aspen is slow to burn, so is used for safety matches and for the structure of sauna cubicles. It is also used in the paper industry. As sawdust and shreddings it is used for packing and animal bedding, and an aspen wood product called *excelsior* is referred to as "wood wool".

**Myth and Story:** The Celts believed the tree's trembling occurred when it was in communication with the Otherworld and the spirits of the dead, with which this tree is strongly associated. A crown or headdress made of aspen was said to facilitate communion with the dead, and crowns of aspen twigs found with ancient burials may have been intended as a message for the dead person, or as a means for them to be reborn more easily. Like all the Ogham, Eabadh is protective. The Greek name for the tree was Aspis, which means a shield, and it was believed that a sprig carried into battle or worn on the head would protect a warrior in the thick of the fray. Scottish Celts believed a leaf placed on the tongue would confer the gift of eloquence. The aspen is yet another tree to have been said to form the cross of Christ – perhaps we should only list trees that have not!

**Magic:** An aspen headdress (as noted above) or an aspen wand can be used in a ritual to invoke the spirits of the dead. Decorate the altar or magical space with leaves and twigs of aspen for rituals of communion with the dead. The tree is also used as a talisman for overcoming obstacles and gaining courage in difficult situations.

**Divination:** From the *Bríatharogam*, it is plain this letter has some connection with water and with fish, perhaps the Salmon of Wisdom which was so culturally important to the Celts and to the Druids. This ties it to Saille – a strongly water-connected *few* which speaks of dreams, magic, inspiration and the spiritual life. But it also has a strong meaning of place, especially sacred places. The meaning of "grove" is that of the sacred space used by Druids both historically and today, their outdoor temple, and in today's parlance the very group of people who meet there (or who might meet virtually). Eabadh speaks of the knowledge and inspiration that can be accessed in such a sacred space, of one's spiritual path and the potential that lies within. Of course, it can also speak of the Wiccan circle, the "place that is not a place in the time that is not a time," and of other sacred places as well; temples, stone circles and even Christian churches. Pagans are aware that most, if not all, sacred places on the Earth are linked by lines of power, that conversations go on between them, exchanges of energies. And does this not remind us of the Wood Wide Web, of the communication that goes on between trees? All things are linked, in pagan belief, all part of the Web of Wyrd or fate. Aspen trees themselves are said to share a common root between a whole grove of the trees, which may arise from the ease with which they send up suckers to replace fallen trees.

Perhaps Eabadh can also speak of the virtual temple used by many practitioners of magic when they are away from home and their own sacred space. The space – whether it is a castle, a forest clearing, a cave or a hilltop – is created by visualisation, oft repeated, and can be stocked with the practitioner's own magical tools and furniture with which he or she is very familiar, so that bringing them into this imagined space is easy.

**Manannan's Bag:** Graves tied this *few* to Manannan's shears, which the shape resembles, and which had once belonged to the King of Scotland. Shears may be used for cutting of course (whether human hair, sheep's wool or cloth from a loom) and the last two uses may bring the meaning of achievement or harvest into this *few*, as well as a sense of the ending of one cycle and the beginning of a new one. Taking the traditional meaning with the meaning associated with Graves's idea speaks of spiritual goals achieved, of a sense of success in ascending on your spiritual way.

This Ogham is not capable of being reversed, although it may lie sideways.

## Visualisation Story

You are entering a sacred grove, perhaps once planted by the ancient Druids. The grove is of oak and aspen but other shrubs and plants have moved in over the centuries and filled in the spaces between the trunks, and swathes of ivy hang down like cloaks. The Moon is full and rising in a cloudless sky and the stars are sharp and bright. You stop for a moment, experiencing a sudden pang of grief as you remember your mentor, who taught you all about using the Moon phases. She died a month ago and you still feel her loss very acutely; you have often felt quite lost and without guidance, but you are determined to carry on in her memory.

You are here because you have reached a milestone in your spiritual life and wish to mark this with a solitary ritual, as you are not affiliated to any group. It is a lonely place and very dark, and you are afraid, despite yourself, knowing that the place is said locally to be haunted. You actually find yourself trembling like Shaggy in *Scooby-Doo*. But you grasp your courage with both hands and advance to the centre of the space. Here you are conscious of a springing of strange energy, your body hums with it and your fingertips all but emit sparks. The fear vanishes, as you begin to appreciate just what this place means and what it can do for you.

Falling to your knees, you call on the ancient Gods you honour, asking for their blessing as you begin your rite of self-initiation. You call your mentor's name, asking the Gods to bless her on her journey and to let her know you will never forget her or the blessing of knowledge she gave you. Then you feel the very lightest touch on your shoulder, as though someone laid a hand there, a touch so gentle you think at first you imagined it. But she is all around you; you even catch a whiff of the perfume she always wore. She is with you: you are not alone.

You complete your ritual and feel the power of the grove enter you, filling you with power and courage.

## *Oir or Or ♦ Riches, Wealth, Being Valued, Triumph.*

This is the diphthong OI, but can represent TH.
Pronounced: OH-ir.
**Tree:** The spindle tree: *Euonymus europaeus*.
**Female**
**Rune:** Berkana and Othila.
**Tarot:** The Ten of Pentacles and the Wheel of Fortune.
**Deity(ies):** Arachne, Athena/Minerva, the Fates, Freyja and Frigga, Neith, Pluto, Sunna, the Valkyries.

**Correspondences:** Colours: gold and silver. Crystals: All precious stones.
**Planet:** The Sun.
**Element:** Water.
**Sabbat:** Imbolc.
**Living Things:** Shiny gold flowers such as celandines, chickens, pigs and cattle.

Thriving on chalky soils, the **spindle** tree is found in open woodland, hedges and scrub, rather than in dense woods, and is an indicator for ancient woodland. A small tree, not usually achieving more than 8-9 metres in height, it is extremely pretty with its jasmine-like flowers which appear in late spring, followed by an abundance of red-orange fruits of an unusual four-lobed shape.

**Range:** *Euonymus europaeus* is found across Europe, and decorative cultivars are popular in parks and gardens, where its smaller size is useful where space is at a premium, notably *E. japonica*. The garden varieties are grown across the world, particularly in Asia and as far south as South Africa.

**Healing Properties:** The spindle tree's leaves and berries are very poisonous, but the tree has been used for liver disorders. The poisonous content of the fruit has been used to repel nits, lice and fleas from children and animals by powdering the dried berries and applying to the scalp.

**Uses:** Spindle wood is extremely fine-grained and hard, so that it is possible to tool it to a very sharp point. This no doubt is why it was traditionally used for the making of spindles for spinning thread, from which it derives its name, but it is also used for knitting needles, clothes pegs, bobbins, tobacco pipes, skewers, arrows, toothpicks and other fine pieces. In the US it is known as the arrow tree, as it was once used for making this weapon. It is little used now, but one of its uses is the making of artists' charcoal. Due to its poisonous nature, the leaves of the spindle were traditionally scattered in houses among the strewing rushes to deter lice, fleas and other insects.

**Myth and Story:** Probably the most famous spindle of all time is that in the fairytale *Sleeping Beauty*, in which the young princess pricks her finger and falls into a 100-year sleep – perhaps a memory of a person long ago who was poisoned by the toxic wood of the spindle. The tree was considered unlucky if brought into the house, perhaps because of its poisonous nature. Yet, because of its Greek meaning (Eu = good or well, onyma = name), it was considered auspicious in some cultures.

**Magic:** Like many ancient skills, the act of spinning is seen as deeply magical and is associated with many Goddesses. In Norse belief, Freyja was the patroness of witches, and the völva, or Norse witch, would carry a magical seidstafr in the form of a distaff, or spinning staff, as part of her regalia and tools. Today, not many people would consider doing their own spinning; but knitting, tatting, crochet and sewing can all be used for spinning magic. Spinning is a useful tool in spells for bringing people together, reuniting folk who have quarrelled, and binding couples who are having difficulties. Spindle wood, to a lesser extent, shares with hazel the ability to dowse. The spindle is protective of the home and family.

**Divination:** The name of this *few* means "gold", so it speaks of money, of riches, of the precious metal with which its name seems to be linked etymologically. The *few* even looks like a cut diamond or other precious stone. In the dim and distant past, women especially were valued for their domestic skills, with spinning being seen as a very desirable ability, and even one that could create riches (as in the folk tale *Rumpelstiltskin*).

Oir can therefore be taken to refer to riches, whether those be material goods, large numbers on the bank statement or riches of some other kind – such as spiritual ones. Drawing it may mean that you will come into some money, or it could mean that others come to value you as you would wish, that you achieve importance in some way, perhaps through your wealth or through the work you do. In either case, it is a positive *few* and by its shape is incapable of being reversed.

The *few* speaks of feminine power, of an influential female person in your life or changing your destiny, as well as referring to groups and communities, those "spun" together by some means.

The spindle tree gets its name because its wood was used to make spindles, weighted wooden spools used by women to spin wool and flax, a common and daylong household task in the days before industrial production of fibres. A woman would often carry her spindle with her wherever she went, using it quite automatically as she got on with other tasks or socialised with other women. This could bring the meaning of women's issues into this *few*, the suggestion that any message is about females in the equation, instead of males. In Greek culture, the spindle – and by extension, the tree – was associated with the Moirai or Fates, who dictated lives by spinning them – Clotho whirling the spindle, Lachesis measuring it out and the last Fate, Atropos, then deciding on a person's time of death by cutting the thread. Spinning and weaving have been associated with many Goddesses, including Athena, Arachne, Freyja, Neith, Sunna and the Valkyries.

If you are seeking clarification, having drawn Ogham *fews* from the main set, this *few* may indicate that their message was to do with your financial situation, or your property – perhaps a better piece of news about a financial difficulty you are experiencing.

**Manannan's Bag:** Graves linked this *few* to the helmet of the King of Lochlann, as its shape might suggest a helmet, the upper triangle, over a face formed by the lower one. In Irish legend, the supernatural Formorian invaders (who fought a savage war with the Tuatha de Danaan) came from Lochlainn or Lochlann, a kingdom under the sea. Such wars tend to be territorial and this could bring the meaning of property or struggles over property and wealth into this *few* as well, or perhaps that of strife with or even conquest of a terrible foe. In Irish belief, the Formorians were inhuman monsters – a fearful foe to come against – yet the Tuatha de Danaan prevailed against them and drove them back from whence they came.

The *few* cannot be **reversed.**

## Visualisation Story

Jake sits at a computer in a makeshift office in a room in his house, staring at the screen at some news he has just received. There is a tap on the door and his partner enters, carrying a cup of tea. He turns and looks at him, a huge smile on his face. The other stops dead.

"No!" he says, slopping the tea over the top of the mug in his excitement.

"Yes!" replies Jake, "and it's more than I hoped." He names a sum that almost causes John to drop the tea altogether.

"Thanks to all our friends who wrote in and offered to speak for you at the hearing," replies John. "They must have had a mail sack the size of the ones in *Miracle on 34th Street*. Serve 'em right for treating you like that just for being gay."

"It's good to have so many loyal friends, and to feel so valued," Jake remarks.

"Well, you did it for them as well," remarks John, "it's a clear warning shot to any company that thinks it can bully and victimise a person for being gay and disguise it as something else."

Jake laughs agreement. "And do you know what I want to do now? Give it all to charity!"

### Uilleann or Uilleand ᚛ Love, Comfort and Contentment, Skill and Knowledge.

This is the diphthong UI, and can also represent PE – remember the Irish Celts did not use the sound P, so this was a later addition to keep pace with the language as it accepted outside influences and changed.

Pronounced WEE-lah.

**Tree:** The honeysuckle or woodbine: *Lonicera periclymenum*, and this *few* is also associated with the beech tree and with the ivy: *Helix hedera.*

**Female**

**Rune:** Othila and Ehwaz.

**Tarot:** The Lovers and the Ten of Cups.

**Deity(ies):** Frigga, Hera, Juno, Vesta/Hestia, all Goddesses of marriage and the home, Gods of knowledge and skill such as Apollo, Hephaistos, Hermes/Mercury and Odin.

**Correspondences:** Colour: pink. Crystal: rose quartz.

**Planet:** Venus.

**Element:** Earth.

**Sabbat:** Beltane and Lughnasadh.

**Living Things:** Roses and scented flowers, cats, dogs, horses.

The **honeysuckle** or woodbine has the most delicious, honeyed fragrance and beautiful golden and pink blossoms throughout its long flowering season. Apart from its blooms, it is an inconspicuous twining plant with green to dark red tendrils and somewhat nondescript foliage that buries itself cosily in a hedgerow or against a wall or fence.

**Range:** Native to the Mediterranean, the US and the temperate parts of Europe, honeysuckle has been taken to many countries, where it thrives in full sun or partial shade in most soils. *Euonymus* species are found in the Americas, across Asia, Africa and into Australia, where some species are so successful as to be considered a pest. "Woodbine", another of its soubriquets, has been applied to sweet-smelling flowering vines across the world, which could also stand in for this Ogham plant.

**Healing Properties:** Honeysuckle was thought to have healing powers and a sick child, for example, might be passed through a ring of honeysuckle tendrils nine times. The plant material would then be cut up and burned. The plant itself is quite poisonous, so should not be taken internally, yet it has been used – by professional practitioners, it must be stressed – for diabetes, digestive problems, urinary tract infections, coughs and colds (it contains salicin), general infections, arthritis and even cancer. Externally, it is useful on irritable, sore and itchy conditions. It is antibacterial. The Bach flower remedy is used for people stuck in the past, who feel the future is hopeless.

**Uses:** Honeysuckle is employed mainly as a decorative vine to hide unsightly outhouses or walls and to bring colour and scent. Many attractive variations have been developed, with deeply coloured blooms and even variegated foliage. There are even species with edible berries (common honeysuckle berries are poisonous) which are grown commercially for food.

Honeysuckle tendrils were once braided together for rope and woven into baskets. Walking sticks formed from wood around which honeysuckle has twined itself, shaping the stick into a spiral, are much prized, and both sticks and wands made in the same way are considered magical by pagans.

**Myth and Story:** This most attractive and perfumed of our native hedgerow plants has inspired poets with its honeyed fragrance and is said to be beloved of the Fae for the same reason. For many poets it has embodied the quality of enduring love and faithfulness, as has the ivy. Both plants grow in a twining way around woody plants and trees, embracing them closely, suggesting love and marriage – and with honeysuckle, also sweetness and a pleasant life. Honeysuckle flowers are most fragrant at night, which continues the idea that they are associated with marriage and the pleasures of the marriage bed, or of lovers' meetings.

**Magic:** Grown around a home or used as a symbol over the door or hearth, it is said to bring good fortune and protect the home and family from ill-luck. It speaks of sunshine and happiness, a "place in the sun", of contentment and marital bliss. Magically it can be used to sweeten life and especially married life, where a couple find themselves at odds. It can also help those stuck in the past and the feeling that the present has nothing to offer and the future is uncertain.

**Divination:** Uilleann speaks of the places where you feel at home and comfortable, for comfort is the watchword of this *few*, comfort of the home, comfort of the family, comfort in your relationship and in your career. All is well, says Uileann's appearance in your casting, your home is safe, your family is well and you yourself are filled with well-earned contentment and have no reason to be anxious or unhappy. As well as domestic bliss, the *few* indicates physical wellbeing, and its strong connection with healing speaks of hope and healing for a person perhaps suffering a long-term condition; or of a speedy resolution of a simple common illness such as the flu.

Uileann means "elbow", and the word is associated with music through the Irish version of the bagpipes, known as Uilleann pipes. The meaning could therefore bring the idea of flexibility and strength into the *few*, as well as artistic expression, particularly through the musical arts.

**Manannan's Bag:** Graves associated this *few* with the hook of the supernatural smith Goibniu, a member of the Tuatha de Danaan who represented among other things the virtue of hospitality. Goibniu, who seems to have been an Irish version of the legendary Welsh smith Gofannon, also brewed a magical ale which conferred immortality on those who drank of it. His skill was mythic and in one story it is Goibniu who makes King Nuada a silver arm to replace the one he has lost in battle – a metal arm which worked as well as the original limb. These stories could bring these qualities of magic, of skill, of wisdom and of kindness, into this *few*.

**Reversed:** The *few* warns of discomfort and something to be avoided, whether this is a health issue or a meeting with someone you very much do not wish to see. This reversed *few* may be a warning that all is not well at home or in your marriage, and it counsels you to take care, take precautions, be on the alert.

## *Visualisation Story*

This Ogham creates a place in the mind: a sheltered and homely cottage where a fire blazes cosily in the kitchen and the rough wooden table is loaded with sweet and tasty things as the housewife prepares to create something wonderful for her family when they come home from work and school. She is not rich in anything but love and happiness, but she knows how to create a wonderful meal from very simple, cheap ingredients: this is her special skill.

Diligently she works away, kneading bread, rubbing and rolling pastry, peeling and chopping vegetables, measuring flour and sugar: most of these ingredients have come from the garden, and she adds things she has grown herself in her own little corner, herbs to give savoury or sweet flavour.

The pot is on the fire and the little clay oven is hot and filled with bread and pasties. The door opens, bringing in a strong fragrance from the honeysuckle that twines around the rustic porch. Shouting and giggling, her children enter, followed by their father. He stands for a moment in the doorway, just looking at the scene, taking in the welcome, the happiness, the warmth and cheer, the scent of delicious food.

## Iphin or Pin ✖ Birth, Rebirth and Health.

This is the diphthong IA but was also used for PH and for P. Pronounced iff-EEN or PEEN.

**Tree:** The gooseberry: *Ribes uva-crispa*. Confusingly, some books associate it with the pine.

**Female**

**Rune:** Berkana and Eiwaz.

**Tarot:** Death and the Ace of Swords.

**Deity(ies):** Aesclepius, Airmed, Apollo, Bride, Isis and Osiris, Juno Lucina, Lugh.

**Correspondences:** Colours: Honey-gold and yellow. Crystals: Black and dark crystals. **Planet:** Venus.

**Element:** Water.

**Sabbat:** Imbolc.

**Living Things:** All perennial spring flowers, birds and eggs, phoenix, snakes.

The **gooseberry** bush is found in cottage and kitchen gardens everywhere, with its bright green leaves that look a little like hawthorn leaves and the fat, green, yellow or pink fruit hiding shyly within their cover, guarded by sharp spines. Although we are more familiar with the cultivated gooseberry, wild gooseberry bushes are found in the UK and Europe.

**Range:** The bush is native to Europe as far as the Arctic Circle and Asia, including the Himalayas, and has been introduced into many other regions as a garden plant and a commercial crop, including Africa and Australia. A century ago, their growing was banned in the US because the plant was found to be a host for a tree disease called "white pine blister". In some states, notably Maine, their growing is still illegal.

Whilst it will not grow in extreme conditions of heat and cold, the gooseberry has many analogies in other countries – other plants that share the name "gooseberry", yet are unrelated, such as the Cape Gooseberry (*Physalis peruviana*) in South America, and the Chinese gooseberry (*Actinidia spp*), now called the kiwifruit and grown in New Zealand.

**Healing Properties:** The fruits have been given to young women just before their monthly menstruation to help with discomfort and the berries are especially beneficial to pregnant women as they help the body absorb calcium, needed for the formation of the baby's bones and teeth. Similarly, it is good for older women, and men, helping to stave off osteoporosis and keep the teeth healthy. Like their close cousins the red- and blackcurrants, gooseberries are rich in health-enhancing vitamin C and were used to break a fever. Gooseberries are said to help with pica cravings during pregnancy. Iphin will help magically with the regeneration of damaged or diseased tissues and can be carried by a sick person to this end, or even inscribed on a plaster cast.

**Uses:** This bush is grown for its juicy if somewhat sour fruit, which is eaten with cream and sugar, made into pies, desserts and jams, used to flavour drinks and used as a sauce for oily fish and rich meats, especially pork.

**Myth and Story:** "Gooseberry bush" was once a crude term for a woman's pubic hair (and may be the origin of the expression that babies are found under gooseberry bushes!) and the plant has been associated with Goddesses of fertility and childbirth. As the child is born from the pain and blood of the mother, so the tender and desirable fruit has to be taken at risk to the hands from this thorny bush.

In common parlance, a third person who insists on intruding when a couple wants to be alone together is called a "gooseberry".

**Magic:** The magic of the gooseberry largely lies in the domain of the cook, but they can be used for healing spells and spells for fertility, using them as a libation and as a symbol of fruitfulness. The thorns from the bush can be used in protective (all thorny plants carry protective qualities) witch bottles and in place of pins for poppets, if you are that way inclined.

**Divination:** Strongly associated with babies and childbirth, also with pain, this *few* speaks of new beginnings, of births and deaths (rebirth into another reality) and the health conditions associated with birth and fertility. It also speaks of releasing past emotions, especially guilt and shame for past actions which cannot now be changed, and accepting your life as it is now, building enjoyment in the here and now, and not wasting regrets on what could have been. It can mean the healing of trauma, as well as physical ailments. Another kind of new beginning, after all.

**Manannan's Bag:** Graves called this *few* Asil's pig-bones, and it does rather resemble a stack of clean-picked ribs. Asil's pigs were magical creatures that could be slaughtered for a meal and eaten, but be found alive and well the next morning, a four-legged equivalent of the magic porridge-pot found in some mythologies. It echoes the idea of the magical pig of Valhalla, Saehrimnir, who was cooked every night for the Gods' supper and was alive again the next day. The pigs also gave good health to anyone who ate their flesh, just as the gooseberry does.

**Reversed:** The letter cannot be reversed. The symbol above includes the ridge, which is not part of the letter.

## Visualisation Story

Felicity puffs and puffs, trying to remember what she learned at the birth class.

"You're doing really well," soothes the midwife, wiping her forehead with a damp cloth. "It won't be too much longer now."

Probably what she says to everyone, Felicity thinks; well not everyone is going through this and a broken marriage at the same time. "Aah!" she gasps as another contraction seizes her.

She remembers her friend, who has three children, telling her she wouldn't notice if a brass band came into the delivery room at this point, but Felicity does see the door open and a nurse put her head in. The head withdraws immediately and she hears whispered conversation outside.

Then the door opens wider and Jamie comes in. Felicity is already gasping from the pain and is in no position to demonstrate her astonishment. They parted acrimoniously four months before and have had little or no contact since then.

Jamie comes into the room and sits beside the bed.

"Why don't you f*** off!" gasps Felicity, in a small gap where she is able to speak. The midwife tuts audibly but doesn't seem surprised. She is used to women swearing at their husbands in the throes of childbirth.

Then suddenly it is all go and the midwife snaps into action, two nurses appear from nowhere, and all Felicity can do is groan and let her body do what it wants to do.

"There," says the midwife sometime later. Jamie is walking about holding his son, a huge smile on his face, but the baby is taken from him and rapidly removed for washing and whatever other mysterious processes take place behind the scenes. The couple are left alone.

"A new life," says Jamie. "Not just the baby, but us. This has made me realise how stupid I was. We had something good, and let a quarrel spoil it. Now this new person has arrived, and it feels like a new life, a new chance."

Felicity smiles and cries simultaneously.

## Eamancholl ▦ Ill-health or Ill-fortune, Travels, Broadening the Mind.

This is the diphthong AE, and can also represent XI.

Pronounced eh-MAN-cul.

**Tree:** The witch hazel (*Hamamelis spp.*) is generally given for this *few*, yet this tree is not native to the UK and a more likely candidate is the wych elm (sometimes called the witch elm or Scots elm) *Ulmus glabra* – a member of the elm family and the only one native to Britain, the English elm being a Bronze Age introduction. This tree has also been called the wych hazel, although it is not related to the *Hamamelis* species. This *few* is also, with Peith, associated with the beech *Phagos sylvatica*, and with the sea, which ties in with Graves's identification of it with Manannan's sea map shirt.

**Female**

**Rune:** Nauthiz and Raido.

**Tarot:** The Chariot and the Four of Swords.

**Deity(ies):** Ceridwen, Hecate, Hel, Arawn and all Underworld Gods, Loki, Odin, Saturn.

**Correspondences:** Colours: Black, dark brown and turquoise-blue. Crystals: Black and dark crystals.

**Planets:** Saturn and Mercury.

**Element:** Water, air and earth.

**Sabbat:** Samhuinn/Samhain.

**Living Things:** Black dogs and pigs, crows and ravens, white flowers.

The **wych elm,** like its cousin the English elm, has the typical asymmetrical leaves, roughly heart-shaped and with a pointed tip, but these are much longer in the wych elm. The tree commonly grows to 30 metres in height and has the classic elm shape, once such an iconic part of the UK countryside, with a round broad crown. It can also be a victim of Dutch elm disease, but the elm bark beetles are not as drawn to it as they are to other species as its tissue contains a chemical compound called alnulin, which repels them.

**Range:** The tree is found from the Arctic Circle down to the Mediterranean and the Middle East, particularly in mountainous regions. Other varieties of elms are found across most of the globe, including Africa, Australia and the whole of North America, but not South America.

**Healing Properties:** Chewing the inner bark of the wych elm was once a popular cure for toothache, and the bark was also powdered and used for a number of complaints, including stomach-ache, diarrhoea and the nerves. Externally, it was applied to wounds and ulcers and used for rheumatic joints. Slippery elm, a substance obtained from a related species in North America, has been used for stomach complaints ranging from constipation to stomach ulcers, and as food for invalids.

**Uses:** The wood has an interesting twisty grain (which in extreme cases is called "burr elm") and is used by craftsmen for decorative items, including furniture and gun stocks, also flooring, bowls and cups, and the timber has famously been used for coffins. Because it does not rot quickly in water, it has been used in ship building and for items such as lock gates and draining boards, which come into constant contact with water. The young leaves in spring can be eaten raw in salads and have a pleasant sharp flavour.

**Myth and Story:** In Norse mythology, Odin created the first man, Askr, from an ash tree and the first woman, Embla, from an elm. The tree was believed to protect from witches (perhaps the origins of its name) and particularly the dairy activity of the household, which was always considered vulnerable to witches and mischievous fairies. Twigs of wych elm were hung around the dairy, and a piece might be used in the butter churn to make the butter form, and also to prevent the fairies from stealing the butter. In some folklore stories an elm rod could be used to beat off the Devil himself!

Along with the yew, elms are associated with death and the world beyond. The Celts associated elms with passages to Annwn or Tir na nOg, such as graveyards and burial mounds. Welsh bowmen made their bows from elm wood rather than yew. In Greek legend, Orpheus, who tried to rescue his beloved wife Euridice from the Underworld, played her a love song – at which an elm tree grew on the spot.

**Magic:** Despite its association with death and the afterlife, elm is used in spells of love and fertility, the wood and bark can even be ground finely and used in an incense mix for this kind of magic. It is suitable for rituals at the Dark Moon, and the twigs can also be used for dowsing.

**Divination:** Perhaps the darkest of the Ogham, Eamancholl does not bring much in the way of comfort when it appears .... interestingly, if you Google it, Google immediately suggests "melancholy" as what you perhaps meant to type. Yes, it speaks of death and endings and also of illness, and the implication may be that the travel it also indicates could be beyond this world. This is frightening for most people, though not for all, and one is prompted to recall the words of Peter Pan: "To die would be an awfully big adventure!" Or it might mean the travel required by a sick person who cannot find the right specialist or treatment near their home and has to go abroad, which brings hope into the reading.

Yet physical death is very seldom suggested by divination and the travels could be the result of one ending – such as a job coming to an end, or retirement, or a marriage being dissolved – and the new adventure that starts when that happens. If you are using the *few* as a scene-setter, it could be indicating travel and movement in your life in some particular area, such as your holidays or a planned move of house or relocation to another country.

Either way, the *few* says that you must end something, whether that is an unhappy marriage, a job that has become stifling or a home you have lived in for many years. It is scary but new beginnings are scary too, even though they are full of hope and joy.

**Manannan's Bag:** Graves identified this Ogham *few* with the Sea God Manannan's shirt, which also served as a map of his domain, the oceans of the world. The cross-hatching of this Ogham symbol could suggest longitude and latitude to the modern eye and of course similar systems were in use for navigation from the third century BCE. So it speaks of travel, with all that implies: adventure, movement, broadening the mind and educating oneself, changing one's home, visiting family, holidays, new horizons, new opportunities.

**Reversed:** The letter cannot be reversed. The symbol above includes the ridge, which is not part of the letter.

## *Visualisation Story*

Dee sits in her armchair by the unlit gas fire for the last time, looking slowly around her little lounge. She looks carefully at each piece of old-fashioned furniture and each ornament, every picture on the walls and every framed photograph on the mantelpiece, as though to fix them in her mind for all time. There are gaps: some of her most precious pictures and knick-knacks have already been packed up and put into boxes.

The door opens and her daughter Sylvia comes in, her car keys in her hand. "Time to go, Mum."

Dee turns her face away.

"Now come on, Mum, you're going to be very happy there, and you know you can't stay on here anymore. Don't you remember: you left the front door open two nights running last week? Anything could have happened if Mr Patel next door hadn't rung me about it."

She helps her mother to her feet and hands her her handbag. Silently, Dee allows her daughter to dress her in coat, scarf, gloves and hat – at 87 she feels the cold, even on a mild day like this.

The journey to Primrose House is short and passes in a blur to Dee, who is holding back tears of sadness and anger. She knows Sylvia and Brian have her best interests at heart, but this is such a wrench, to leave the home she has lived in for more than 40 years.

"Here we are," Sylvia says brightly, turning in at the entrance and parking on the small area of tarmac in front of the home.

The front door opens in welcome and a short, plump woman in a blue cardigan smiles them in. "You're going to like it here, dear," she whispers to Dee. The first impression Dee has is flowers: vases full of colour and perfume on every surface. The second is light and warmth. After the dinginess of her little house, this place is filled with sunlight from the large windows and as warm as even she could wish.

Sylvia disappears with the suitcases and blue-cardigan-lady takes Dee through to a large but cosy lounge. Three elderly ladies look up from their game of Monopoly.

"Oh look," says one, "another player for us. Come and join us, dear!"

By the time Sylvia comes down from her mother's room, Dee is almost too busy to look up and say goodbye. Sylvia smiles, then leaves the house and goes to sit in her car, where she bursts into tears of thankfulness, guilt and sadness.

## Peith ▬ The Sea and Travel, Sea Mysteries, Learning and Wisdom.

This is the soft P or PH sound.
Pronounced PEH or PETH.
**Tree:** The beech tree: *Phagos sylvatica*.
Peith is clearly related to Beith, the first Ogham, and may have replaced the earlier Iphin, which was originally called Pin, as the letter P.
**Female**
**Rune:** Laguz and Raido.
**Tarot:** The Chariot and the High Priestess.
**Deity(ies):** Hermes, Odin, Ogma, Mercury, Thoth, Gods of knowledge and inspiration, Neptune/Poseidon.
**Correspondences:** Colours: Light blue, orange and brown. Crystal: Agate.
**Planets:** Mercury and Neptune.
**Elements:** Air and earth.
**Sabbat:** Alban Elfed/Mabon.
**Living Things:** Owls, wading birds and birds that migrate, fish, especially salmon and eels.

The **beech** is a familiar woodland tree with smooth, sinewy branches and oval, deeply ribbed leaves which turn a rich red-brown and stay on into the winter, not being shed until the new leaves are ready to sprout. Beeches can achieve a height of over 40 metres and have a wide spreading canopy and visible surface roots. Whilst the wild beech is familiar, many people will be better acquainted with the copper beech, a variant grown in parks and gardens for its luxuriant purple foliage.

**Range:** The beech is native to Europe, Asia and North America, but has been introduced to Australia. Australia also has two analogous trees, the evergreen myrtle beech (*Nothofagus cunninghamii*) and the Antarctic beech (*Nothofagus moorei*). These southern beeches are found across the Southern Hemisphere and were once believed to be members of the *Fagaceae*; however modern science has proved they are genetically unrelated.

**Healing Properties:** Water gathered from the hollow of a beech tree is said to be a powerful ingredient of a spell to increase one's beauty, and the sap and leaves have been used in the treatment of dry skin conditions such as psoriasis and eczema – it is tied to skin health and beauty by the Doctrine of Signatures. It has been associated with snakes, due to the sleek, sinuous appearance of its branches and roots, and this brings the meaning of magical healing of illness or of poison into this *few*, as the snake has long been associated with medicine. The Bach flower remedy is for people who need give up their overactive egos and have less arrogance and intolerance toward others.

**Uses:** Beech timber is hard and straight-grained and has a number of uses in construction, including the manufacture of plywood, furniture manufacture and items such as kitchen cabinets and parts for musical instruments. Its wood was also used in the making of books: its name in German, "buche", is etymologically related to the word for book, *buch*. It is also closely tied to the food industry, its wood being used for smoking meats and in beer casks, and it is an excellent firewood. It is popular as a hedging plant, particularly due to its winter retention of leaves, which are attractive and give privacy. Beechwood is pulped to produce the cellulose fibre modal, which is used in clothing. The nuts, which are called beechmast, have traditionally been a staple for free-range pigs, but can be eaten by humans, although they are very small and rather bitter.

**Myth and Story:** The tree is important in mythology and folklore, and shares with hazel the gift of inspiration, given to anyone who eats of its nuts. The tree has been associated with knowledge and wisdom (not least because its bark was used by the ancient Celts for writing on) and with the keeping and protection of knowledge. The beech tree has always been regarded as feminine, perhaps due to the smoothness of its bark resembling a woman's skin, as a female counterpart to the male oak, and has shared the epithet "Lady of the Woods" with the birch.

**Magic:** The tree is generally associated with the working of magic and with the flow of inspiration and it has a connection to the Druid mantra *Awen*. Wishes, especially for healing, can be inscribed on a length of beech wood, which is then buried in the ground: as the wood rots, so the spell takes effect. The tree's strong connection with books makes it useful in magic to spread learning or messages, or for someone seeking help in learning a new subject, perhaps starting a new course. Slips of beech wood would be useful to create lamens (items on which magical words or sigils are inscribed) and are one of the woods traditionally used for creating an Ogham set.

**Divination:** Very little information can be found about this late letter, which shares the beech tree with Eamancholl; in fact the two Ogham *fews* seem to overlap quite a bit in their messages and areas of influence. But where Eamancholl includes quite negative meanings, Peith seems to be about more positive ideas: learning, travel, adventure and uncovering mysteries.

The beech tree is closely associated with Ogma Sunface himself, who is said to have written his newly invented letters upon its wood, so this *few* may act as a binding for the letters, bringing them all together and helping make sense of their messages. The *few* may refer to the writing down of facts and of history, so that memories may be retained, or of the written wisdom of books (and websites). It could even speak of the dangers of adhering too closely to old ideas, of moving on and leaving behind old prejudices and preconceptions, of thinking for yourself, striking out a new line, or it could be a hint to learn from the past, rather than disregarding the lessons of history. This *few* is associated with the sea, which of course also holds old memories and hides ancient mysteries.

**Manannan's Bag:** Graves seems to associate it with the whalebone in Manannan's bag, which continues the message of the foregoing letter about travel and the sea.

**Reversed:** The letter cannot be reversed. The symbol above includes the ridge, which is not part of the letter.

## *Visualisation Story*

Bea leans against the kitchen sink and takes several deep breaths. Her daughter has just arrived, as the happy din of laughter and chatter in the hallway tells her, but Bea is not yet quite prepared to go out and meet her.

Don puts his head around the door at last, and calls her into the lounge, and Bea is obliged to go, though she takes her time drying her hands, taking off her apron and carefully folding it before laying it on a chair. Still she stands, looking down at the apron: it is one Isobel bought her years ago for Mother's Day..... Bea jerks away her gaze, before tears can gather in her eyes, and heads off out of the kitchen.

Izzy is holding forth in the lounge, watched admiringly by her father and brothers. She looks so beautiful and delicate, so fragile even, that Bea feels a sob gathering in her throat, and suddenly she has to leave the room, almost as soon as she has entered it.

Don makes to go after her, but Izzy lays a hand on her father's arm. "Let me," she says.

In the kitchen Bea is wiping her eyes and sniffing, with her back to the door in case someone comes in. Izzy goes to her mother and puts her arms around her.

"Mum..." she begins, then realises she does not know what to say.

"Izzy...the South Pole!" wails her mother, "why does it have to be somewhere like that? I thought you might marry that nice Shergold boy and settle down!"

"I know, Mum. It's hard to explain. But it's a whole world to explore, so much knowledge tucked away in the ice. And the continent influences the whole world, you know...weather and all sorts. We'll study the penguins too, and there are even bugs... bacteria and all sorts that you don't find anywhere else. There are things deep down in the ice, from millennia ago...."

She is talking to herself now, her voice filled with wonder and her eyes looking into the distance. Slowly Bea stops crying as she listens and begins to understand what this adventure means for her child, who is so very different to herself.

# Briatharoghams

Just as runic scholars have relied on the rune poems to crack the divinatory and magical meanings of the runes, so Ogham students have a body of knowledge they can refer to, giving words about each Ogham letter which can be examined for meaning.

As with the rune poems, there are three *Bríatharoghams*, or "word oghams", lists of all the letters with a short *kenning*, a punning description, giving clues to their meanings. Dating from the Old Irish period, the *Bríatharogham Morainn mac Moin* and the *Bríatharogham Maic ind Óc*, are both found in the ancient *In Lebor Ogaim*, the *Book of Oghams*, a manuscript written in Old Irish and preserved in the National Library of Ireland, and also referenced in the fourteenth century *Book of Ballymote*. The third, the *Bríatharogham Con Culainn*, is only found in later manuscripts, from the sixteenth and seventeenth centuries.

Here is a table of the *Bríatharoghams*, with their original kennings translated by the Ogham scholar, Professor Damien McManus. Yes, we agree they look pretty cryptic! But, like the rune poems (of which there are also three), meaning can be wrested from them with a bit of thought and meditation. We have included all the Ogham *fews* used in magic and divination, with the translated meanings of their names and their kennings, and also the six more generally known of the *Forfeda*, the six additional Oghams which are not generally so used.

| Ogham | Ogham Name Meaning | Bríatharogham Morainn mac Moin | Bríatharogham Maic ind Óc | Bríatharogham Con Culainn |
|---|---|---|---|---|
| Beith (birch) | Birch tree | Withered foot with fine hair | Greyest of skin | Beauty of the brow |
| Luis (rowan) | Flame or herb | Lustre of the eye | Friend of cattle | Food of cattle |
| Fearn (alder) | Alder | Vanguard of warriors | Milk vessel | Protection of the heart |
| Saille (willow) | Willow | Pallor of the dead | Food of bees | Beginning of honey |
| Nion (ash) | Branch fork or wave | Establishing of peace | Boast of women | Boast of beauty |
| Uath (hawthorn) | Horror, fear | Assembly of packs of dogs | Paling of faces | Most difficult at night |
| Duir (oak) | Oak tree | Highest tree | Handicraft of a craftsman | Most carven handicraft |
| Tinne (holly) | Iron bar | One of three parts of a wheel | Marrow of charcoal | One of three parts of a weapon |
| Coll (hazel) | Hazel tree | Fairest tree | Sweetest of nutshells | Sweetest of trees |
| Quert (apple) | Bush or rag | Shelter of a madman | Substance of an insignificant person | Remains of clothing |
| Muin (vine) | Neck, trick or love | Strongest in exertion | Proverb of slaughter | Path of the voice |
| Gort (ivy) | Field | Sweetest grass | Suitable for cows | Sating of multitudes |
| Ngetal (reed) | Killing | Food for a leech | Raiment of healers | Start of killing |
| Straif (blackthorn) | Sulphur | Strongest red (dye) | Increase of secrets | Seeking of clouds |
| Ruis (elder) | Red | Most intense blushing | Reddening of faces | Glow of anger |
| Ailm (silver fir) | Pine | Loudest groan | Beginning of an answer | Beginning of calling |
| Onn (furze) | Ash tree | Wounder of horses | Smoothest craftmanship | Equipment of warrior bands |
| Ur (heather) | Earth | In cold dwellings | Propagation of plants | Shroud of a lifeless one |
| Edad (poplar) | Aspen | Discerning tree | Exchange of friends | Brother of birch (?) |
| Idad (yew) | Yew tree | Oldest tree | Fairest of the ancients | Energy of an infirm person |

| Ogham | Ogham Name Meaning | Bríatharogham Morainn mac Moin | Bríatharogham Maic ind Óc | Bríatharogham Con Culainn |
|---|---|---|---|---|
| THE FORFEDA | | | | |
| Eabadh | Unknown | Fair swimming letter | Upbraiding of a sick person | Fairest fish |
| Or | Gold | Most venerable substance | Fairest form | |
| Uileann | Elbow | Sweet-scented tree | Great elbow | |
| Iphin | Thorn | Sweetest tree | Wonderful taste | |
| Eamancholl | Twin of hazel | Groan of a sick person | Groan of a sick person | |
| Peith | Birch, soft P | | | |

Now what on Earth is all that about? The kennings do not appear to have the slightest relevance to the Oghams, yet it is possible, even at a second glance, to see some meanings here and there. Is aspen the "discerning tree" because of its trembling habit? Does elder have a red face because of the hue of its berries and of its leaves in late autumn? Yew can certainly be the oldest tree, as we have seen; hazel has the sweetest of nuts and oak has some claim to being the highest tree. Reeds live by the waterside, so might well be associated with leeches and willow certainly has the grey pallor of a deceased person. Yet, like the rune poems, the meanings are not obvious and must be studied and thought about to extract any meaning. The Ogham was a sacred alphabet to the Druids and would not be written about in a way likely to give away its secrets lightly to outsiders.

### Sandie Coombs

I am a mother of three wonderful children and grandmother to eight. I have lived in North Cornwall since 2001. I am a Druidess and have been a member of The Order of Bards, Ovates and Druids since 2005.

I have had fictional work published in the Touchstone magazine. I also write poetry.

I began studying the Ogham in 2005 and have a Masters' Certificate in Celtic Reiki. Since that time, I have used the Ogham in many different areas of my life including the healing of plants, trees, animals and humans.

My other mystical interests also include Wicca, Astrology, Tarot, Sacred Numerology and Geometry.

I am currently studying Wicca under the watchful eye of a very learned and loving High Priestess. I feel very blessed to have been given this opportunity to add more ancient knowledge to my learnings within the old ways and also share ancient wisdom within the wider community. Gerald Gardner and Ross Nichols were friends. Therefore, pathways intermingled with one another are more beneficial as far as I am concerned.

Love and Blessings within the sacred trees of our Mother Earth. May their roots ground you. Their trunks stabilise you. Their branches reach out to hold and surround you. May their leaves nourish and fill your body with their healing aromas and vital oxygen which gives you life. Blessings upon our trees.

### Diane Maxey

I hail from the Derbyshire Peak District, which is steeped in myths and magic (if you know where to look), Celts and even a few Norse ancestral influences, I'm sure. I have always been drawn to nature – the land, sky and water both above and below – and its healing energies.

From my childhood I knew my working life would always be in healing; consequently from 1970-2014 I trained, then worked as a nurse, then a midwife. My passion was always in midwifery. I worked as a midwife for 30 years and as a community midwife for the last 20 years before retirement.

My path to true paganism was late in coming, partly due to my Christian upbringing, but my psychic abilities were always "bubbling along" in the background.

On retiring to the Southwest, I found my path with the help of my dear friend and mentor Wendy, and am currently a Second Degree Wiccan Priestess studying for my Third Degree.

I love growing herbs, trees (the small varieties!) and flowers – nurturing them, learning their uses and magical properties, which has led to my involvement with this project with Wendy and Sandie.

## Wendy Trevennor

A former journalist, Wendy lives in Cornwall with her husband, their son and a despotic cat. A great-grandmother, a Cornish speaker, a keen WI member and WI cookery judge, she is a lifelong Wiccan and leader of a coven of witches. She has written two previous books on magic and divination: *Witchstones* and *Runes Rebooted*, both published by Green Magic.

Lightning Source UK Ltd.
Milton Keynes UK
UKHW021424131222
413865UK00012B/368